MY FIRST PET RABBIT

Mastering Rabbit Care for Kids and Teens

Ellyn Eddy

LP Media Inc. Publishing
Text copyright © 2024
All rights reserved.

No part of this book may be reproduced or transmitted in any form or by any means, electronic or mechanical, including photocopying, recording, or by an information storage and retrieval system — except by a reviewer who may quote brief passages in a review to be printed in a magazine or newspaper — without permission in writing from the publisher.

For information address
LP Media Inc. Publishing
30012 Variolite St. NW
Princeton, MN 55371
www.lpmedia.org

Publication Data
Ellyn Eddy
My First Pet Rabbit — First edition.
Summary: "Mastering Rabbit Care for Kids and Teens"
Provided by publisher.
ISBN: 978-1-961846-13-5
[1. My First Pet Rabbit — Non-Fiction] I. Title.

Table of Contents

Introduction 5

Chapter 1
What Is a Rabbit? Should It Be Your Next Pet? 7

Chapter 2
So Many Options! A Rainbow of Rabbit Breeds 18

Chapter 3
A Match Made of Fluff: Finding Your Perfect Bunny 35

Chapter 4
Home Sweet Habitat: Rabbit Housing and Equipment 47

Chapter 5
Feeding a Rabbit 58

Chapter 6
A Day in The Life of a Bunny: Everyday Rabbit Care 67

Chapter 7
In Sickness or Health: Keeping Your Rabbit Well 75

Chapter 8
It's Playtime! How to Handle, Train, and Bond with Your Rabbit 85

Chapter 9:
Take Me Out to the Rabbit Show 95

Chapter 10:
Rabbits and Your Future: The Impact of Rabbit Keeping 105

Appendix: Note for Parents and Teachers 111

Appendix: Resources for Further Learning 113

Introduction

Have you ever felt surrounded by rabbits? When I was growing up, I watched Bugs Bunny cartoons before school. I played with my stuffed bunnies when I got home, then settled into bed with a Peter Rabbit story. I wrote my own tales about the wild rabbits that gathered at our birdfeeder every winter. And when spring came, I begged my parents for the bunny-themed merchandise that popped up all over the craft store shelves.

We see rabbits so often in our culture that we might feel like we know everything about them. We might think that keeping one is no big deal. Maybe it's just like caring for a cat or dog.

But real rabbits aren't like cartoon bunnies that can get into crazy mischief without getting hurt. They aren't like plush rabbits that you can stick in a box once Easter is over, either. Real rabbits are social, adventurous, sweet, and surprising.

They're also delicate. For example, foods that are harmless to you—like an avocado—can kill rabbits. Noises or shadows you don't even notice can set a bunny's instincts to red alert.

Rabbits have very different needs than pets you may have had before, like dogs, cats, fish, or even guinea pigs. This is why it's super important to read everything you can about bunny care before you bring a rabbit home.

But don't worry—I wrote you a book!

Hi! My name is Ellyn, and I bet we'd be great friends. Because if you're reading this book, you probably love rabbits as much as I do.

I got my first rabbit when I was eleven and it changed my life. I joined a 4-H club so I could meet other people who had rabbits and I jumped into learning everything about these precious animals.

Pretty soon, I was showing my rabbits at the county fair, winning awards, and coaching younger kids in the hobby. Coaching turned into writing, and writing turned into a career in publishing that I'm still building today. I met my current best friend because she also raised rabbits. And my very first date with my now-husband was at a rabbit show.

Your journey will be different. Maybe you'll become a vet, or maybe you'll turn your passion for animals into a business. Or maybe you'll just use the happiness that bunnies give you to brighten others' lives.

No matter where the rabbit trail leads, I hope you'll find each day better with a bunny by your side.

What is a Rabbit? Should It Be Your Next Pet?

What Is a Rabbit?

Everyone knows that rabbits are furry little animals with adorable eyes and funny-looking feet—but did you know they also have superpowers? Here are a few incredible facts about bunnies that you can use to impress your friends:

The world record longest jump ever by a rabbit was **9 feet, 9.6 inches** long.

Rabbits can run **30 miles per hour** and jump over predators like foxes or coyotes.

Rabbits have almost **360-degree vision** and can see high above their heads.

Rabbits produce **200 to 300** poop pellets every day! This doesn't even include the poops they eat! (More on this later, don't worry.)

The Scientific Classification of Rabbits

Here's one more little-known fact: rabbits aren't rodents!

Pikas are squeaky little egg-shaped critters that live in the mountains.

Scientists who study animals divide all living creatures into groups based on how similar they are to each other. Rabbits (and hares) have so many differences from rodents like mice, guinea pigs, and rats that they get their own "order" called Lagomorpha. We call them "lagomorphs" (pronounced LAY-go-morfs).

"Lagomorphs" are divided into two families: rabbits and hares are in one family, called "Leporidae," and pikas are in another. (Pikas are squeaky little egg-shaped critters that live in the mountains. Sound adorable, right?)

RABBITS vs. HARES

Rabbits	Hares
Young are born helpless (blind, hairless).	Young are precocial (born with fur, eyes open).
Live in burrows and form social groups.	Live above ground, generally solitary.
Smaller in size compared to hares.	Larger than rabbits.
Shorter legs and ears.	Longer legs and ears for running fast.
Have shorter hops and bursts of speed.	Can run fast in long sprints and leap farther.

Within the family "Leporidae," there are 29 different species of rabbits around the world. A species is a group of animals that can have babies together and only choose mates within their own group.

All pet rabbits belong to the species *Oryctolagus cuniculus*. You don't need to try to pronounce that word since nobody really uses it in everyday conversation, but it means that all pet rabbits are the great-grand-bunnies of wild rabbits from Europe.

North American cottontail rabbits are a different species from European wild rabbits. This means that if you live in North America, your pet bunnies cannot have babies with the wild rabbits running around the local park.

Rabbits in the Wild

Rabbits live in a range of habitats in the wild. For example, the riverine rabbit lives along seasonal rivers in the Karoo desert of South Africa, while the itty-bitty pygmy rabbit of the Western United States lives in the Rocky Mountains.

RIVERINE RABBIT

American cottontail rabbits live under shrubs or brush and don't actually dig burrows. The folktales about rabbits living in holes are based on European wild bunnies, which dig extensive underground tunnels and live in communities called "warrens."

So, since our pet rabbits are descended from European rabbits, we're going to focus on the Oryctolagus cuniculus species for most of this book.

PYGMY RABBIT

Rabbits and Humans

Throughout history, the rabbit has fascinated many cultures around the world. The Japanese, for example, imagine a rabbit making mochi on the face of the moon. The ancient Egyptians had a hieroglyph in the shape of a hare that meant "to exist."

Rabbits must have had a terrifying reputation in medieval Europe because artists in the Middle Ages often drew rabbits as archers or swordsmen hunting humans!

We don't know exactly when people started domesticating rabbits—that is, catching them and controlling their breeding. In fact, recent research into rabbit genetics tells us that it probably happened slowly over many hundreds of years.

The ancient Egyptians had a hieroglyph in the shape of a hare that meant "to exist."

WHAT DOES "DOMESTIC" MEAN FOR RABBITS?

Domestic rabbits are those bred by humans over many generations to live as pets. This process took hundreds of years, making them different from their wild relatives.

We do know that ancient people across the globe hunted rabbits for food and sport. In the early centuries of the Roman Empire, rabbits were transported from Spain all around the empire for food. During the Middle Ages, religious monks kept rabbits in walled gardens, letting the bunnies run and breed freely within the walls.

By the 1500s, people had started to keep rabbits in smaller hutches and control their breeding. This led to an explosion of new rabbit fur types and colors. White, silver, red, and blue—each region in Europe developed its own bunny variety with pride. For example, long-haired rabbits, called angoras, probably first came from the mountains of Eastern Europe. But when they made it to England, King Henry VIII declared Angora rabbits a national treasure!

By the 1800s, Europeans had developed dozens of different breeds of rabbits and began to show them off at fairs and competitions. They had Flemish giants weighing 18 pounds. They had English lops with an "ear span" as long as your arm. Some of these rabbits were cruelly treated since their owners only cared about winning at shows — not the rabbit's comfort or wellbeing. However, rabbits had also become common farm animals, where they were usually loved and cared for by children.

Hares / Rabbits from the Johnson's household book of nature, 1880

What is a Rabbit   11

Modern Rabbit Keeping

Rabbit breeding reached peak popularity in the early 1900s when thousands of rabbits were exported from Europe to the United States and Canada. Organizations like the American Rabbit Breeders Association (ARBA) and the British Rabbit Council wrote "standards" that governed rabbit shows, and people began to keep rabbits in wire cages. Used for show, fur, and meat, most rabbits weren't considered pets in this period, but there were a few exceptions.

American Rabbit Breeders Association

British Rabbit Council

We might not like to think about people eating rabbit meat, but many bunnies served a noble cause by keeping families alive during World Wars I and II. The rabbits lived off scraps that humans couldn't eat from "Victory Gardens," and their manure was used to fertilize the gardens.

And although we're even more uncomfortable thinking of rabbits as laboratory animals, the research done on bunnies in labs has saved countless human lives. Did you know that thyroid disease was discovered by feeding rabbits tons of cabbage? Or that rabbits are used to produce monoclonal antibodies even today?

Rabbits as Pets

In modern times, most bunnies are kept in happy homes where they are pampered, protected, and welcomed into the family. Cages have gone out of style; many pet rabbits are trained to use a litter box and enjoy free run of the home.

> "Owning a rabbit is a rewarding experience because you get all the benefits of having a pet, like a dog, without the hassle of walks. They're fun, loving, and with care, they become part of the family."
>
> — **Stephanie Cardine**, Lusters Lops

Rabbits can be registered as emotional support animals, comforting people who are going through a hard season. Some organizations use rabbits as therapy animals and train them to visit hospital patients who need a bit of fluffy joy in their day.

Many kids also love to show off their bunnies at county fairs or local 4-H events. These kids carefully brush their bunnies, practice handling them, and feed them the very best food so they'll be all ready for the big day. The life of a 4-H rabbit looks different from the life of a pampered indoor pet, but both types of bunnies are usually cared for with equal compassion and pride.

WHAT IS 4-H?

4-H is a national youth program where kids learn life skills through hands-on projects, often in areas like animal care, farming, and science. Many participants show their bunnies at local "county fairs," which are community events featuring contests, exhibits, and farm animals. These fairs are a fun way for kids to showcase their hard work and dedication.

Rabbits as Superheroes

Of course, we all hope for a future in which lab experiments will never have to be done on animals. We should be working toward a world in which everyone who touches a rabbit will treat it with dignity and kindness.

But it's helpful to look back at history and realize the impact rabbits have had. Rabbits have provided food for millions of people. They've been key to the medical progress of the recent century. Bunnies have been a spark of happiness for many people in times of darkness, whether through folktales or real-life fluffy bunny snuggles. Rabbits are true superheroes who wear many capes.

We should never underestimate the gift that rabbits have been to humanity, and we should reward our bunnies with the best of care.

ARE YOU READY FOR A BUNNY?

> "**M**ake sure you are prepared for a long-term commitment. Rabbits can live up to 10 years, and they need daily attention and a large, clean living space. Handling them frequently builds trust and a stronger bond."
>
> — **Eva M. Wells**, author of *Continental Giant Rabbits in USA*

Since rabbits are superheroes with very particular needs, you need to make sure a bunny is a good fit for your family before you bring one home.

First, let's remember all the reasons why you'd probably love keeping bunnies as pets:

- They're cute. Like, gotta-have-one-now, "IT'S SO FLUFFY" kind of cute.
- They're fun to watch as they play, rest, and nibble their day away.
- They show they love you by licking or nuzzling you and flopping on the floor at your feet.
- They can learn tricks like leaping over hurdles or standing on their hind legs.
- They live six to 10 years, so you have plenty of time to build a friendship.
- They're great pets for kids. If you're at least seven or eight years old and don't mind hard work, you can probably take care of a bunny without an adult helping too much.
- You can join a 4-H club and meet other friends who love their rabbits.

But before you go bunny shopping, we have to look at the less glamorous side of rabbit care. Rabbits are like every other good thing—they come at a cost. Having a rabbit means you might not get to do some other things you enjoy.

You should ask yourself the following questions to make sure you're really ready to become a rabbit owner. These are a lot of questions, but they're all very important.

- ☐ Do I have at least 30 minutes to spend with my rabbit every single day?
- ☐ Can I feed my rabbit before school every day, even if that means waking up earlier than I do now?
- ☐ Am I ready to get my hands dirty and clean poop and pee off the litter box, the cage, my bedroom floor, and wherever else it ends up?
- ☐ Is anyone in my family allergic to rabbits?
- ☐ Do I mind the smell of livestock or hay?
- ☐ Who will pay for my rabbit's cage, food, and veterinary bills?
- ☐ Do I know someone who can take care of my bunny when I go on vacation—and can I pay that person if I have to?
- ☐ Do I understand that some rabbits don't like to be held and cuddled, and am I okay with relating to my bunny in a way that makes it comfortable?
- ☐ Do I have a safe place to keep my rabbit that is out of the weather and protected from predators and loud noises?
- ☐ Does my family have other pets like dogs, cats, or large birds that might frighten my rabbit? Can I keep my bunny away from them all the time?
- ☐ Since rabbits can live six to 10 years, how old will I be when my rabbit passes away? Will I still want to care for a bunny when I'm older and busy with other things?
- ☐ How will I handle the sadness if my rabbit gets sick or passes unexpectedly?

"**A** rabbit absolutely makes a great pet for a child who is looking for a different experience to a dog or a cat. Rabbits teach responsibility and can help a child focus on routine while building a strong bond with a pet who is not the typical choice. Rabbits do not require much by means of care as they are one of the most low maintenance pets, but they do give back so much more in affection. Rabbits have their own unique personalities and figuring them out is half the fun and it is the most rewarding part to rabbit ownership!

— **Krissy Rezzelle**, Whispering Wilds Rabbitry

I know this is a lot to think about, and I'm not trying to scare you off. I'd love to welcome you to the world of happy bunny owners! But I know that you, your family, and your rabbit will all be happiest if you plan for the more difficult parts of caring for a living, breathing, adorable pet.

So Many Options!
A Rainbow of Rabbit Breeds

"**D**on't buy just any rabbit, do your research, find what breed or breeds you might want, and have everything ready before bringing a rabbit home. Join the American Rabbit Breeders Association for additional guidance and support."

— **Pamela Fitzgerald**, Hoppy Trails Rabbitry

All right! So, it's time to take your first step on the trail of adventures in rabbit ownership. Before you hop off to the pet store, ask yourself, "What kind of rabbit will fit in best with my family?"

There are over 50 rabbit breeds in the United States and many more worldwide. Each breed has a unique feature—maybe a color pattern, fur type, or personality—that makes it different from other rabbits.

Some breeds are popular no matter where you live. Others are less common. Try not to set your heart on one particular breed or color. You might not be able to find your exact dream bunny in your area.

But since rabbits of different shapes and sizes have different care needs, it's helpful to learn about your options. Let's take a look at some of the most interesting and popular rabbit breeds today.

WHAT IS A BREED?

A breed is a group of rabbits that share specific characteristics, such as fur texture, size, or temperament, passed down through generations. Each breed has unique care needs based on its physical traits and personality. Learning about different breeds helps you find the rabbit that fits your lifestyle.

THE LITTLEST BUNNIES

The smallest rabbits are called "dwarfs." Dwarf bunnies weigh only about three pounds when full-grown. They are popular pets because they're easier to pick up than larger bunnies. They can live in smaller cages. They also eat and poop a lot less than bigger breeds. And when they shed, it doesn't look like a giant hair monster swept through your house!

But dwarf rabbits may have health problems that larger bunnies don't have. Because of their ball-shaped heads, their teeth might grow crooked. If you get a dwarf rabbit, check its teeth carefully to make sure the top incisors are fully overlapping the bottom ones.

If you are planning to breed your rabbit, you should also know that, sadly, fewer dwarf rabbit babies survive than babies of larger breeds. For these reasons, some people consider breeding dwarf bunnies to be unethical.

NOTE ON WEIGHTS

Weights given in this chapter are not ARBA standard weights. They are more practical weights, rounding up or down a bit from ARBA weights, which are complex and different for bucks/does.

NETHERLAND DWARF

Weight: 2–3 pounds

Fur type: Short, thick coat

Colors: Many color groups

Personality: It's variable—some are wonderful, and others aren't.

POLISH

Weight: 2–4 pounds

Fur type: Short, silky coat

Colors: Solid-colored, white, and spotted

Personality: Funny, energetic, and sometimes feisty

LIONHEAD

Weight: 3–4 pounds

Fur type: Short, thick fur on the body with long hair around the head and rump

Colors: A wide selection of colors, but they can't all be shown.

Personality: Usually good-tempered, with exceptions

FROM DWARFS TO GIANTS, OH MY!

Rabbit breeds that weigh between four and seven pounds as adults are considered "small" breeds. These are easy to handle and often have friendly personalities. They don't have the same health problems that dwarf bunnies do.

Medium-sized rabbits are sometimes called "commercial" breeds. They weigh eight to 11 pounds at eight months of age. People who raise meat rabbits prefer this size.

Lastly, a few rabbit breeds are absolutely huge. They can weigh up to 20 pounds or more! That's as big as a toddler and larger than most house cats!

SMALL: DUTCH

Weight: 3–5 pounds

Fur type: Short, silky coat

Colors: Black, chocolate, gray, or other colors—always with white markings

Personality: Usually friendly and great for pets

COMMERCIAL: CHAMPAGNE D'ARGENT

Weight: 9–11 pounds

Fur type: Short, thick coat

Colors: Born black and grow silver-white hairs as they grow older

Personality: Average to good

GIANT: FLEMISH GIANT

Weight: 13–22 pounds

Fur type: Short, thick coat

Colors: Chestnut, sandy, gray, and others

Personality: Happy and chill

Giant Bunnies Have Big Needs

Imagine a friend walks into your home. Your pet comes over to check them out. Your visitor assumes it's a dog at first but then does a double-take and exclaims,

"IT'S A GIANT RABBIT!"

This scenario sounds like fun, but giant bunnies are more work than regular-sized breeds. They need to live in large enclosures with solid floors because they are too heavy for wire cages. These enclosures are a lot of work to clean because giant rabbits produce so many droppings!

Can kids pick up giant rabbits? I've seen them do it! It's possible if you practice, but giant bunnies are very, very strong. If they kick or struggle, they can injure themselves and give you deep, long scratch marks that will hurt like nobody's business. Trust me: I have scars. 😉

Fur Type and Length: Breeds with Unique Coats

Most adult rabbits have fur that's between one inch and one and a half inches long. They have long, stiff guard hairs that protect their soft, warm undercoat from dirt and water. Most bunnies don't need to be brushed very often because rabbits clean their fur with their tongues several times a day.

Angora rabbits look like fluffy clouds. They have long hair called "wool" that can grow an inch every month! They are beautiful, but taking care of an Angora is an intense and time-consuming job. They need to be combed and trimmed often to stay healthy.

On the other paw, you have rex rabbits. Bunnies with rex fur have unusually short and dense coats. Their guard hairs aren't much longer than the underfur, and all the hairs stick upright from the skin. This creates a plush "velveteen" texture. You'll never forget petting a rex.

MINI REX

Weight: 3–4 pounds

Fur type: Rex (short, plush fur)

Colors: Many colors and patterns

Personality: Usually very sweet and funny

JERSEY WOOLY

Weight: 2–4 pounds

Fur type: Short, fluffy wool that's about two inches long and easy to care for

Colors: Many color groups

Personality: Relaxed and easygoing

ENGLISH ANGORA

Weight: 5–7 pounds

Fur type: Beautiful, airy, and silky wool that can grow to eight inches long and needs lots of care

Colors: Many color groups

Personality: Calm

Ears Up or Down: Lop Rabbits

Many of the bunnies you see on packages around Easter time are lop rabbits—bunnies with floppy ears. Many lop rabbits have "crowns" of fur and cartilage on the top of their heads that push the ears down by their faces. When a bunny's ears aren't fully "lopped" but stick out to either side, say it has "airplane ears."

> "Holland Lops are a popular small breed with generally good temperaments for first-time owners. When choosing a rabbit, don't be hesitant to ask the rabbitry owner questions about the rabbits. They are around them every day and know the rabbit's personality and if they would make a good pet."
>
> — **Gordon McRae**, Creekside Rabbitry

HOLLAND LOP

Weight: 3–4 pounds

Fur type: Short, thick coat

Colors: Many color groups

Personality: Usually active and friendly

ENGLISH LOP

Weight: 9–12 pounds

Fur type: Short coat

Colors: Many color groups

Personality: Fair to average

AMERICAN FUZZY LOP

Weight: 3–4 pounds

Fur type: Fluffy, easy-care wool that's two inches long

Colors: Many color groups

Personality: Silly and relaxed—great pets

Colors: Breeds with Unique Patterns

Some rabbit breeds come in only one color. Others come in a whole rainbow. Some have unique color patterns that aren't found in other breeds. We call these "marked" breeds.

Some rabbits of marked breeds are born as "sports"—that is, babies that don't look the way the breeder wanted. You can't show these bunnies, but you can rescue them and give them a great life as a pet.

TAN

Weight: 4–5 pounds

Fur type: Short, slick coat

Colors: Black, blue, chocolate, or lilac with fiery red markings

Personality: Very active—best for experienced handlers

ENGLISH SPOT

Weight: 5–8 pounds

Fur type: Short, silky coat

Colors: White with spots of various colors

Personality: Energetic

DWARF HOTOT

Weight: 2–3 pounds

Fur type: Short, thick coat

Colors: Pure white with a colored ring around each eye

Personality: Variable—some are friendly and some not so much

PERSONALITY: BREEDS WITH DISTINCT PERSONALITIES

One of the most important factors in picking a good pet rabbit is personality. Some breeds—like the Himalayan, Mini Rex, and Silver Fox—almost always have friendly personalities. Some, like the Britannia Petite, are more hyper. Rabbits of almost any breed can make good pets if they come from a breeder who handles their rabbits often.

HIMALAYAN

Weight: 3–5 pounds

Fur type: Short, silky coat

Colors: White with markings on nose, ears, feet, and tail that get darker in cold weather

Personality: Very relaxed and docile—don't mind handling

BRITANNIA PETITE

Weight: 2–3 pounds

Fur type: Short, slick coat

Colors: Chestnut agouti, white, black, and others

Personality: Intense—not for beginners

SILVER FOX

Weight: 9–12 pounds

Fur type: Thick, fluffy coat

Colors: Dark-colored with white hairs that increase with age

Personality: Known as the "teddy bears" of the rabbit world

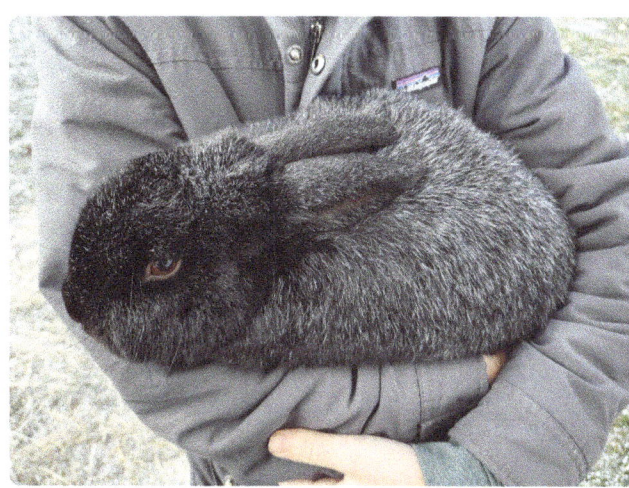

Photo Courtesy of Alison Westermann

Purebred vs. Mixed Breed

As you look at these beautiful bunny photos, remember that there are also many lovely rabbits whose parent breeds are unknown. We call these "mixed-breed" rabbits. You usually can't show mixed-breed rabbits, but they can be happy house rabbits.

Bunnies whose parents were of the same breed for at least three generations are called "purebred" rabbits. Purebred rabbits should come with a "pedigree" or a chart that shows their parents and grandparents. You might need to ask the breeder for the pedigree because they don't always include it when they sell pet rabbits.

Where can you find a good rabbit breeder? I'll give you some tips on finding your perfect bunny in the next chapter!

3

A Match Made of Fluff: Finding Your Perfect Bunny

Besides a rabbit's breed, you'll have to make other decisions about which bunny to bring home. You'll also have to decide whether you should get an adult or a baby rabbit and a boy or a girl. You'll need to find a good place to buy or adopt your rabbit from.

Should You Get a Baby Rabbit or an Adult?

Most people imagine bringing home a baby rabbit that is so small it can fit into their cupped hands. But this is a scary idea from the bunny's point of view! A rabbit that small will probably think the human took him away from his mother to make him into a bunny sandwich!

Baby bunnies stop drinking their mother's milk when they're six to eight weeks old. During this time, their digestive systems are changing very quickly.

When they are learning to eat hay or pellets instead of milk, any extra changes—like moving to a new home—can make them very sick. After they are weaned, or taken from their mothers, they should have at least a month in the place where they were born with the same caretaker before moving to a new place.

THE EIGHT WEEK RULE

In many states, it is against the law to sell a bunny that's less than eight weeks old. But it is safer for the rabbit if you wait even longer.

In fact, there are good reasons to get an adult rabbit as your first pet. Adult bunnies are much stronger than babies. They are less likely to get sick after you bring them home. The seller can tell you what the rabbit's adult personality is like. And if you plan to get your rabbit "fixed" at the vet, your bunny will be already old enough for the surgery.

Avoiding the Unexpected

One time my friend showed me a tiny bunny she bought at a pet store. She was told it was an eight-week-old Netherland Dwarf. It was so small, it fit into the pocket of her hooded sweatshirt! But I had seen a lot of baby Netherland Dwarfs—and this did not look like one to me. It also looked younger than eight weeks, no matter what breed it was.

Even though it was sold so young, this bunny was lucky and survived. In fact, it did great! It grew out of my friend's sweatshirt pocket, out of its cage, and didn't stop growing until it weighed 13 pounds! That's as heavy as a bowling ball! It was definitely not a dwarf bunny!

When you get a rabbit that is already six months old, you don't have to wonder what size it will be as an adult. Most rabbits reach their adult weight between six and eight months of age.

Baby Rabbit vs Adult

Pros

- Easier to bond with at a young age.
- Can be trained from the start.
- Grows up knowing you as their caregiver.

- Already has an established personality.
- Likely house-trained already.
- Requires less supervision during training.

Cons

- Needs more training and socialization.
- More delicate and requires constant care.
- Can be unpredictable as they grow.

- May take longer to bond with a new owner.
- Harder to break bad habits learned earlier.
- Older rabbits may have health concerns.

Bucks and Does

Just like deer, a male rabbit is called a "buck," and a female rabbit is called a "doe." Both boy and girl bunnies make good pets. I think females are more snuggly—but can also be more timid and territorial. Bucks are funny, but they like to mark their territory by flinging pee across the room. (I've been hit in the face before! Yuck!)

When you bring your rabbit home, ask a vet or adult who has experience with rabbits to check your bunny's gender. It's very hard to tell whether baby rabbits are girls or boys. When I bought my first rabbit, the breeder told me it was a boy, but it turned out to be a girl. Many people have purchased two rabbits they thought were the same gender, only to find babies in the cage a month later! Oops! Here's my advice: **if you bring home a baby rabbit, check its gender every month until it is an adult.**

If you don't plan to breed your rabbit, you can take it to the vet to get neutered. This will make your bunny less territorial. It might make him or her more friendly and more interested in bonding with humans.

> ### TERRITORIAL
> Territorial behavior in rabbits means they may aggressively defend their space or belongings, such as their cage or toys, from others.

How to Check a Rabbit's Gender: Step-by-Step

1

Hold Your Rabbit Gently: Place your bunny on its back or hold it so its bottom faces you, keeping it calm and safe.

2

Find the Area: Look near where the poop comes out (the anus).

3

Gently Press: Lightly press around the area in front of the anus.

4

Look for Clues: A boy rabbit will have a small bump, while a girl will have a long, thin slit.

5

Check Every Month: Keep checking as your rabbit grows to be sure.

Do Bunnies Need Friends?

Should you bring home two rabbits so your bunny can have a friend? Do rabbits like to have company?

In my opinion, rabbits can do well alone or with another bunny. Single rabbits often bond more easily with their owners. They will be more interested in playing with you or licking you if they don't have a rabbit companion.

Rabbits, especially ones that aren't neutered, like to have their own space. I find that they enjoy having other rabbits in the area but not in their own cage with them.

However, rabbits that are neutered may "bond" with each other, groom each other, and play with or sleep with each other. Neutered rabbits can live in the same space together quite happily.

Finding Your Perfect Bunny

WHERE CAN YOU FIND A RABBIT TO BUY OR ADOPT?

Where should you get a rabbit? Easy, right? The pet store?

Actually, it's not that simple. Most big pet supply stores in the United States, like Petco, don't sell live rabbits. You can find some privately owned shops that sell rabbits, but a pet store isn't the best place to get a bunny.

Most bunnies sold in pet stores were taken from their mother when they were too young. They may have caught diseases from the other rabbits in the store or from the customers who handle them. They are always stressed. And stress is very unhealthy for bunnies.

It Matters Where You Get Your Bunny

The place where you buy or adopt your rabbit is the most important choice you make before bringing your bunny home. It's more important than which breed you get or whether you get a boy or a girl.

If you get your rabbit from a good place, your bunny will be healthy. The seller (or shelter workers) will know your rabbit's personality and maybe its family history. They will answer your questions about rabbit care. You'll also be able to contact them if you have problems in the future.

But if you get your rabbit from a dirty pet store, your bunny will come with problems. I wish I could say this wasn't true. I wish I could say that you might be lucky—but I've seen people buy sick pet rabbits too many times.

It's not just pet stores. Many unsavory breeders sell rabbits just to make money. They don't care about the animals or the success of the new rabbit owner.

You should stay far away from a breeder or pet store if you see any of the red flags listed below.

WARNING SIGNS OF AN UNETHICAL BREEDER

- They don't thoroughly answer your questions. A good breeder should seem excited that you want to become a bunny owner!

- They brag a lot about what they have accomplished with their rabbits. (For example, how many shows they have won.) It's okay if they mention some winnings, of course. But they should focus on you and your success, not brag about themselves.

- They claim they have never had sick rabbits. (Every breeder deals with disease at some point. The important thing is how you handle sickness when it happens.)

- They don't seem interested in the rabbit as an individual. They should be able to tell you about its parents, its personality, its health history, etc.
- They won't meet you in person but try to send you the rabbit with a handler instead.
- They ask you to send money before you see the rabbit in person.
- They handle the rabbit roughly, or the bunny seems afraid of them.
- The rabbit has dirty feet or a dirty tail.
- They are rude or dismissive about anything!

If you meet a breeder to buy a bunny, but something gives you bad vibes, just say "no thank you" and leave. **It's okay to walk away from a bad situation.** You don't need to bring the rabbit home to "rescue it." Unfortunately, if you do pay a bad breeder and bring the bunny home, you are simply supporting them in mistreating more rabbits.

WINNING ISN'T EVERYTHING

Winning at shows does not prove someone takes good care of their rabbits, or that they will sell you a winning rabbit. One time, my dad drove 300 miles to pick up a rabbit for me from a breeder that won at a national show. That rabbit had a disease called "snuffles" when we got it home. It also came in last place in every show where I entered it. This breeder took advantage of the fact that she had a reputation and we were newcomers. She sold us an expensive bunny that didn't meet expectations.

Finding a Good Breeder

So, how do you find a breeder you can trust?

There are good rabbit breeders out there—there really are. There are high-quality people who love their animals and take very good care of them. These are the people you need to find.

The best way is to ask for recommendations. Call your local extension office (you can do an Internet search for the number) or talk to 4-H leaders and ask them for breeders' names. You can also contact a local representative of ARBA or the national club for the rabbit breed you want.

> "I always tell new rabbit owners to physically visit the breeder if possible. It gives you a chance to see how the rabbits are raised, check the cleanliness of the facility, and ensure the breeder cares about the well-being of their animals."
>
> — Gina Williams, Rabbit Habitat

You can find rabbits for sale by going to rabbit shows or by searching on the Internet. However, when you find a breeder online, you will have to trust their word that they take good care of their bunnies. Here's a list of helpful questions to ask a breeder.

- What do you like about your rabbit breed? Do you think it's a good breed for kids?
- What is this bunny's personality like? What are his parents like?
- What happens if the bunny gets sick after I bring him home?
- What are some challenges you've dealt with in your rabbitry?
- What is the most helpful advice you would give a new rabbit owner?

Make sure you ask these questions before you fall in love with a particular rabbit the breeder has available! The breeder should be very happy to answer your questions and not push you to buy or talk only about themselves.

DISQUALIFICATION

A disqualification from competition can be a white spot, a broken toe, or anything else that makes a rabbit unable to compete in a show.

If you are planning to show your rabbit, you'll want to ask more questions. Ask what the bunny's strong points or faults are. Ask if it has any disqualifications from competition. Ask the breeder to show you what the judges look for in that breed of rabbit. You can learn so much by talking to a good breeder!

Animal Shelters and Rabbit Rescues

If you don't plan to show your rabbit and are just looking for a pet, then an animal shelter is a great place to go! Here are some pros and cons of adopting from a rabbit rescue or animal shelter.

PROS OF ADOPTING FROM A SHELTER

- The rabbits have been handled and are used to people.
- The rabbits are vaccinated and inspected by a veterinarian, so you know they are healthy.
- The rabbits may be already neutered, so you won't have to pay for that.
- The adoption fee is very reasonable.
- You are saving a bunny that needs a good home.

CONS OF ADOPTING FROM A SHELTER

- Rabbits in shelters may be several years old already.
- You can't show or breed a shelter rabbit after it has been neutered.
- The shelter may not have the breed or color you want.
- They won't be able to tell you about the rabbit's family history.

Rabbit Health Checklist

Finally, the big day comes. Maybe you arranged a meeting with a breeder. Or maybe you're going to a shelter. It's the day you're planning to bring bunny home!

There's one more important step to take. When you see the rabbit in person, you need to check it over carefully to make sure it's healthy before you agree to buy it. Chapter 7 of this book includes a checklist that will help you recognize any sign of illness.

If you can, bring a friend with you when you go to see a rabbit—a friend who is used to handling bunnies. This friend can check the rabbit for you. They won't be afraid to look at a bunny's teeth and toenails, and they will notice symptoms of sickness that you might miss.

If you don't have a friend experienced with rabbits, a 4-H club is a great place to meet one! 4-H clubs are groups of kids that have a common interest in rabbits or other animals. Clubs have adult leaders that are happy to help if you are new or have questions. Joining a 4-H club before you get a bunny is a great way to prepare for rabbit ownership!

"When picking your rabbit, there are several things you should watch for. Whether you choose to get your rabbit from a shelter or a breeder, make sure you take the time to get to know the rabbit you're adopting. The bunny should look healthy. It should have bright eyes, a clear nose, well aligned, short teeth and a clean bottom. It shouldn't feel bloated or bony. It should act alert and energetic. It should be well socialized and should not panic or show aggression when it is picked up."

— **Heather McCurry**, High Country Holland Lops

Home Sweet Habitat: Rabbit Housing and Equipment

You've picked out your new bunny! Now, where is it going to live? In your heart, of course. But the best way to show your rabbit how much you love it is to provide a safe and comforting habitat for it to hang out in.

Ideally, of course, you'll plan all this out before you bring your rabbit home. Grab a pencil and paper, and as you read this chapter, draw or jot down some rabbit setup ideas that you like. As a kid, I diagrammed my rabbit space with as much excitement as if it were a fairy tale castle, and my drawings helped me explain to my family what I had in mind when we built the hutches.

> "One big mistake is underestimating the amount of space rabbits need. They aren't just cage animals; they need room to hop and explore to stay happy and healthy."
>
> — **Heidi Decker**, Hickory Way Farm

Outdoor Hutch or Indoor Living?

You've discovered by now that taking care of a small creature involves making a lot of decisions for it. (Wait 'til you try parenting—but that's a different topic.)

The first decision to make about rabbit housing is whether your bunny will live inside or outdoors. Maybe you've already made up your mind about this. Maybe it was part of your negotiations with your family about getting a pet. ("Can I get a bunny?" "Well, only if it lives outside!")

Or maybe you live in a high-rise apartment with no outdoor yard. Maybe you want to keep your bunny in your bedroom. A rabbit can be perfectly happy there! One of rabbits' superpowers is that they can live happily inside or outside. But you must understand the pros and cons of each situation and get the right supplies to keep them secure and comfortable.

Advantages of Keeping Rabbits Indoors

+ There is no risk of predator attacks (except from a dog or cat) or theft.
+ There is no risk of freezing, overheating, or weather-related injury.
+ You don't have to go out in extreme weather to care for your rabbit.
+ Your rabbit can't run away if it gets out of its cage. (Though they often won't run away when they live outside, either.)
+ Indoor rabbits usually live longer due to their less stressful lives.
+ It's easier to bond as your rabbit becomes a part of your hour-by-hour life.

There's a third option that bridges the gap between keeping bunnies inside and outside—a pole barn or shed. If set up right, a barn or shed can give your bunny the protection of living indoors while keeping your home free from dander and smells. Most breeders that have lots of rabbits keep them in a "bunny barn."

Advantages of Keeping Rabbits Outdoors

+ Rabbits enjoy natural light and smells.
+ There are fewer sudden or scary household noises for rabbits.
+ Ventilation is excellent—which is crucial for rabbit health.
+ It does not create a mess or odors inside your home.
+ There is less exposure for people with allergies.
+ You don't have to bunny-proof your house.
+ You have enough space to keep multiple rabbits and breed them.

> "If you plan to keep your rabbit outside, make sure to give them access to a shaded area in the summer and proper bedding to keep them warm during the winter. A secure pen will protect them from predators."
>
> — Pamela Fitzgerald, Flop-A-Lop's Rabbitry

How to Keep a Rabbit Safe Outside

Before I got my wonderful rabbit shed, I kept my rabbits in a wooden hutch in our backyard. My parents didn't grow up with animals and didn't realize the perils that could befall the bunnies outside—so we made a lot of mistakes. When I tell you that the wind can blow your hutch upside down or that raccoons can pull bunnies' toes off through the cage bars, I'm not just being dramatic. It's awful, but I've seen those things happen. To prevent these horrors, your outdoor rabbit cage must check these boxes:

- The bottom of the cage must be raised three or more feet off the ground, too high for dogs and coyotes to reach.

- The floor should be solid wood or wire over a solid drop tray. No exposed wire floors.

- The cage door must be locked—not just latched—so that raccoons and small children can't open it.

- The cage should protect the bunny from rain, snow, and direct sunlight but not be so closed in that it blocks airflow.

- The cage and hutch must be made of strong materials. Rabbits can chew through two-by-four lumber, and predators can tear through cheap wire (like poultry netting).

If you Google "outdoor rabbit hutch," you'll find loads of cages for sale that are completely unsafe for outdoor rabbits. They are made of flimsy wire, set directly on the ground, and they have cheap latches.

Unfortunately, the only foolproof way to keep a rabbit safe outside is to build a strong hutch yourself or keep the cage in a closed barn. The barn must be fully secure. I had raccoons sneak in through a six-inch crack under the door and wreak devastation.

Keeping Outdoor Rabbits in Weather Extremes

Many people wonder if rabbits can live outdoors in the winter. I grew up in frigid northern Michigan, and my bunnies did fine outside all winter long. I ran a heater or took rabbits indoors when temperatures dropped below 10 degrees Fahrenheit. They handled temperatures above that well as long as they had high-protein food, fresh water, and shelter from direct wind.

Bunnies hate the heat more than the cold. Since they're wearing a fur coat full time, they can quickly overheat in temperatures above 80 degrees Fahrenheit.

Basically, whenever it feels hot enough to run through a sprinkler, you need to check on your outdoor rabbit often. Keep the hutch in the shade, make sure it gets lots of airflow, and give your rabbit a frozen water bottle or chilled ceramic tile to keep it cool.

How to Keep Rabbits Safe Indoors

If you decide to keep your bunny inside, you won't have to worry about weather extremes and wild animals. But you'll have a different set of challenges. You'll need a solution for droppings and a large space for your rabbit to play.

> "Rabbits explore the world with their mouths, so it's essential to rabbit-proof your space. Make sure wires are covered, and there's nothing harmful within their reach, like wood, drywall, or carpet."
>
> — **Brieanna Camper**, Brie's Bunny Barn

Perils for indoor rabbits come in the form of larger pets, poisonous houseplants, and electrical wires that look so tempting to chew.

Rabbits need to constantly gnaw something to stay happy and healthy. If not stopped, an indoor rabbit will take chunks out of furniture legs and baseboards and may chew and eat carpet. Ingesting carpet can create a life-threatening blockage in a rabbit's tummy.

The simplest solution is to keep your rabbit in a large cage or exercise pen most of the time. You can take it out to play when you can watch it and prevent any destructive behavior. But some people prefer to litter-train their rabbits and let them run free in their house or a specific room. If that's your plan, you'll need to "bunny-proof!"

How to Bunny-Proof a Room in 6 Steps

1. Flooring. Use gates to keep rabbits off carpets and slippery tile floors. (They hate slippery footing!)

2. Cover baseboard and trim molding.

3. Cover furniture legs and make sure the bunny can't get stuck under sofas.

4. Conceal and enclose ALL electrical cords. (A product at the hardware store called "split loom tubing" works great for this.)

5. Keep fabrics like curtains, bed blankets, and dirty laundry out of reach— unless you want holes in them!

6. Remove hazards like ant baits, mouse traps, or houseplants.

Supplies You Need for a New Rabbit

Most of the supplies you will need for a rabbit are the same, whether you keep your bunny inside or outside.

Let's make a rabbit equipment shopping list!

THE ESSENTIALS

- Cage
- Litter box or drop tray
- Transport carrier
- Food dishes
- Water bottle
- Nail trimmers
- Grooming comb or brush
- Litter or bedding
- Hay
- Pellets

OPTIONAL ITEMS

- Hay rack
- Nesting box
- Toys
- Tunnels or agility equipment

Types of Cages

Rabbit cages come in many different designs and different materials.

All-wire cages are the cleanest. Poop falls right through the wire floor into a collection tray, which you can empty every few days. Wire cages are also very secure and protect rabbits from predators. The disadvantage is that wire floors can be rough on bunnies' feet. Rex-furred breeds particularly struggle with wire floors.

Hybrid cages are widely available on Amazon and websites like Chewy.com. They are partially made of wire and partially of wood or plastic. Some of these are made with low-quality wire that won't protect rabbits from predators. Bunnies can also chew through the cheap wood components. These cages may have areas that are difficult to clean. They work best for indoor, potty-trained rabbits that pee or poop in a litter box instead of in the cage.

Homemade all-wood hutches are usually used outside. They protect rabbits from predators well. But since wood absorbs urine, wood hutches need frequent cleaning, or they'll build up a harmful, nasty smell. My favorite solution for outdoor rabbits is an all-wire cage made of high-quality galvanized wire that's raised and secured by a DIY wood hutch.

Are Cages Good or Bad for Rabbits?

Many people think it's cruel to keep rabbits trapped in cages. But that's not how bunnies see it. Bunnies think of their cages as hideaways, not prisons. Rabbits are prey animals. They believe that everything is out to get them, and they love having a safe cage to call home.

You certainly should let your rabbit out to play every day! But after an hour or two of running around, you'll feel your bunny pulling for its cage as you carry it back.

If you have a house rabbit, you can leave the cage door open when you are home so your rabbit can come and go at will. But you do need a cage, exercise pen, or other enclosure to keep your bunny safe while you're not supervising.

How Big Should a Rabbit's Cage Be?

A rule of thumb is one square foot of floor space per pound of body weight. This means that a four-pound rabbit should have a cage that's at least two feet square, with enough height to stand up on its hind legs. Rabbits that rarely get to come out and play should have more space in their cages.

> "Make sure your rabbit's housing is in a quiet place, away from loud noises or predators. They are prey animals, and a calm environment helps them feel safe and secure."
>
> — **Ken Marks**, Some Bunny Loves U Rabbitry

Setting Up a Rabbit Restroom

Most bunnies pick a corner of their cage to use as a bathroom. This means that you can easily potty train bunnies if you convince them to use a litter box instead of going on the floor.

Fill the litter box with bedding that's safe for rabbits to ingest—like shredded paper. Since bunnies explore the world by chewing on it, they will eat some of their litter. Clay or silica cat litter can kill a bunny that eats it.

If you use wire cages, you'll need a solid plastic or metal tray to slide under the cage and catch the droppings. If you have a solid wood hutch, you'll want to fill it with bedding that you can scoop out every few days —again, shredded paper works great.

WOOD SHAVINGS AND SAWDUST PELLETS

Are wood shavings or sawdust pellets safe bedding for rabbits? Most vets consider hardwood aspen shavings safe for bunnies. There's less agreement about bedding made of softwood cedar or pine. Some rabbit experts believe it is harmless. Others claim that the chemicals that create the rich smell of cedar and pine wood cause stress to rabbits' livers.

Food Dishes and Water Bottles

Bunnies love to dig in their food bowls and, if they can, may toss the whole thing across the cage. I like to use heavy-duty food bowls that clip onto the cage to prevent these behaviors. You may also want a wire rack or bag to keep your bunny's hay off the floor.

An adult rabbit should have a thirty-two-ounce water bottle. Rabbits can drink out of a bowl, but bottles are better. Bottles keep the water free of bugs, debris, and algae.

Do You Need to Buy Toys?

Rabbits' favorite ways to play include chewing, digging, and jumping. You can create many toys for rabbits yourself. For example, you can fill a cardboard box with shredded paper for them to dig in. If you'd like to buy your rabbit toys, they enjoy chew sticks and bells.

Grooming Tools and Toys

Short-haired rabbit breeds don't need much grooming. At a minimum, though, you'll need to get a comb and nail trimmers. We'll go into more detail on rabbit grooming in Chapter 6.

Where Should You Buy Rabbit Equipment?

A pet store may have some of the supplies you need, but you may have to look for others online. If you go to a rabbit show, you can find dealers selling wire cages and other equipment specially designed for keeping and breeding rabbits.

You can also look on resale websites. If you find a secondhand cage that's still in good shape, make sure to sanitize it and inspect it carefully before you use it.

5

Feeding a Rabbit

I was once asked to write an article about "Can rabbits eat carrots?" When I told my husband this, he thought it was a joke. "Of course, rabbits eat carrots!" he laughed. And, thanks to Bugs Bunny, that's what most people believe.

For the record, rabbits can eat carrots—as a treat. But rabbits shouldn't eat carrots every day any more than you should start each morning with a cupcake! Instead, rabbits have another incredible superpower: they can live on grass alone. Human digestive systems can't break down grass and pull nutrients from it, but rabbits can.

Rabbits are able to digest woody plant material—called cellulose—because of their highly specialized gut. Their amazing digestive system begins with teeth that must grind, grind, grind all day, or they'll grow too long for a bunny's mouth. Rabbits are grazers like sheep and cows. Rather than eating a few large meals as we do, they need to nibble on fibrous

plants throughout the day to keep their teeth and bowels healthy. But unlike cows, rabbits only have one stomach.

Instead, rabbits have a huge organ at the beginning of their large intestine, called a cecum, that ferments their food with billions of beneficial bacteria. The bacteria in the cecum adapt to the kind of food that the rabbit is eating—and they're healthiest if it's high-fiber grass.

Rabbits are strict herbivores, which means they can only eat plants. They do not have the right bacteria to digest meat, dairy products, or even large amounts of sugary plants like fruit—or carrots.

Sorry to start the chapter with a science lesson, but knowing how a rabbit's digestive system works is foundational to taking good care of a bunny. Rabbits' superpower, the ability to eat grass, comes at a cost. It means they can only eat high-fiber foods like grass or hay. They cannot safely "cheat" their diets. Feeding the wrong thing to a rabbit can cause a toxic response from its gut bacteria, with terrible consequences.

What Should Rabbits Eat?

Hay is the bedrock of a healthy rabbit diet. Hay is simply cut, dried green grass. Since hay is up to 30% fiber, it will keep a rabbit's digestive tract chugging along happily. Your rabbit should have fresh, good-smelling grass hay in its cage around the clock.

Most rabbit owners also feed their bunnies pellets. Animal nutritionists developed pellets to have the exact ratios of fiber, protein, fat, vitamins, and minerals that rabbits need to live. Pellets are basically nutrition bars for rabbits. However, they can have all the right things on paper but be made of sketchy ingredients.

People who breed and show their rabbits usually feed their bunnies mostly pellets, giving hay as a supplement for fiber. Many pet owners do the reverse, feeding their rabbits 90% hay and vegetables and only giving a few pellets to make sure their bunnies get trace minerals.

No matter whether they eat mostly hay or mostly pellets, adult rabbits need diets that are 20 to 25% fiber, 12 to 15% protein, and 3 to 4% fat. (Nutrition labels for animal feed give ranges of crude nutrients in percentages instead of exact grams as human nutrition labels do.)

Hay There

So, let's talk about hay. There are two main categories of hay: grass and legume. Grass hays are high in fiber and lower in protein, energy, and calcium. Grass hays are healthy for all rabbits. Common grass hays include Timothy, orchard grass, and oats.

ALFALFA

TIMOTHY HAY

Legume hays, like clover and alfalfa, are made from plants in the pea family. They contain more protein than adult rabbits need. They are also high in calcium, which can cause kidney stones and nasty "bladder sludge."

Pregnant females and young rabbits need extra protein and can have some alfalfa hay along with their Timothy. But if you see red urine or a sticky, milky substance (excess calcium) in your rabbit's pee, these are signs that you should reduce the legume hay it's eating.

> "A rabbit's digestive system is incredibly sensitive. Hay is essential to keep it functioning properly and prevent issues like GI stasis, which can be life-threatening."
>
> — Melissa Rowan, Rowan Rabbitry

Pellets

There's a huge range of quality in commercially produced rabbit pellets. Some—the expensive ones—are made of mostly hay. You can order these online or find them in small packages in some pet stores. But be careful; you can also find poor-quality pellets in pet stores. Avoid pellets that contain corn, fruit, or colored bits.

Bulk pellets come in huge 50-pound bags at the animal feed store. They usually don't contain grass hay at all. They are made of cheaper ingredients, like soybean hulls, wheat middlings, and alfalfa meal. They are fortified with vitamins and minerals. These formulas check the boxes for rabbits' nutrient needs, and breeders report their rabbits thrive on premium brands of pellets. But they aren't the most natural way to go.

"**N**ever underestimate the importance of fresh water and a balanced pellet diet. Avoid too many treats and make sure your rabbit always has access to hay to keep their teeth healthy."

— **Jessica Waldron**, Pine Acres Poultry and Rabbit Farm

Vegetables

And what about veggies? Should rabbits eat a salad every day? Again, there are different opinions on this, and you can choose an option that works for your rabbit. If you feed your rabbit mostly hay and not pellets, then fresh vegetables will help fill out its vitamin intake. If you feed mostly pellets, then vegetables aren't strictly necessary.

You should rotate the vegetables you give your rabbit and not offer the same thing every day. Moderation is key. Too much cabbage can give your rabbit gas. Too much spinach can cause kidney stones.

Never feed your rabbit veggies that are squishy and on the edge of rotting. It's not a rabbit's job to clean up the lettuce that sat in the fridge for the last two weeks! However, bunnies can eat your fresh veggie scraps (like carrot peels) left over from meal prep. They can also eat parts of some vegetable garden plants (like squash and broccoli) that humans usually skip.

Fresh Grass

Should you cut grass for your bunny to eat? Rabbits can eat grass, clover, and dandelion from your yard as a treat. But there are a few risks to feeding it regularly. Rabbits can get parasites (harmful bugs that live in their guts) and catch diseases from wild rabbits by eating fresh grass, especially if it's wet. Many lawns are also sprayed with chemicals that aren't healthy for your bunny.

How Much Should You Feed Your Rabbit?

As you can see, breeders, veterinarians, and pet experts have different opinions about the best diet for rabbits. Some emphasize the benefits of pellets; some push for using fresh vegetables. But they all agree on one thing: rabbits should have grass hay in their cages all day long. Phew, finally, harmony!

Rabbits prefer to eat in the morning and in the evening. But your bunny will adjust to whatever schedule you select for it. The important thing is to feed it at roughly the same time every day so your rabbit will learn the routine. Here are some different feeding plans that can work for bunnies. Choose one plan for your rabbit and stick to it.

Mostly Pellet Diet for Adult Rabbits

- Dwarf breeds — 2 to 4 tablespoons of pellets per day
- Small breeds — 1/4 cup of pellets per day
- Medium breeds — 1/4 to 1/2 cup of pellets per day
- Large or giant breeds — up to 1 cup of pellets per day, or as much as keeps your rabbit in good condition
- Free-choice Timothy, oats, or orchard hay
- Green veggies are recommended but optional

Mostly Hay Diet for Adult Rabbits

- Free-choice Timothy, oat, or orchard hay
- 1 to 2 cups of rabbit-approved leafy vegetables once per day, rotating which veggies you offer
- Dwarf breeds — 1 tablespoon of pellets per day
- Larger breeds — 1/4 cup of pellets per five pounds of body weight
- If you give pellets in the morning, give vegetables in the evening, or vice versa.
- Aim for your rabbit to eat 80% hay, 15% veggies, and 5% pellets.

Keep an eye on your rabbit's weight and adapt these schedules to your rabbit's needs. Always introduce new foods gradually.

And Then There Are Treats

Bunnies will gobble up starchy or sugary treats—but they can't handle many of them. (Remember, our goal is not to upset a rabbit's gut bacteria!) Young rabbits who have recently been weaned should avoid treats completely.

Older, stable bunnies can have a one-inch cube of fruit or a few berries daily as a treat. Check out the list below of safe and unsafe rabbit fruits and veggies.

Safe Vegetables, Herbs, and Fruit for Rabbits

Remember, offer everything in moderation! Introduce new foods slowly.

Vegetables marked with an asterisk (*) are high in oxalic acid, so they should be limited and rotated with other veggies.

- Arugula
- Basil
- Beet greens*
- Bell peppers (any color)
- Blackberries
- Blueberries
- Borage
- Broccoli (especially leaves)
- Brussels sprouts*
- Cabbage (including relatives like bok choy)
- Carrot tops*
- Carrots
- Celery
- Cherries (remove pits)
- Cilantro
- Clover*
- Cucumber (including leaves)
- Dandelion (all parts)
- Dill (fresh)
- Fennel
- Green beans
- Kale
- Kiwi
- Melons (including the rind)
- Mint
- Mustard greens*
- Papaya
- Parsley*
- Peaches
- Pears
- Pea greens and pods
- Pineapple
- Plums

- Pumpkin (including rind and seeds)
- Radish leaves*
- Raspberry leaves
- Raspberries
- Romaine lettuce
- Spinach*
- Sprouts*
- Strawberries
- Summer squash (zucchini, yellow squash, including leaves)
- Swiss chard*
- Turnip greens*
- Watercress
- Wheatgrass

Human Foods That Rabbits Should Not Eat

These foods may be toxic or harmful to rabbits.

- Avocados
- Beans (kidney, fava, any starchy legume)
- Cereal, crackers, or baked goods
- Chocolate
- Corn
- Dairy, meat, and animal products
- Garlic
- Houseplants (all)
- Iceberg lettuce
- Leeks
- Nuts and peanuts.
- Onions
- Potato or tomato leaves
- Rhubarb
- Some garden flowers (tulips, daffodils, etc.)
- Some herbs
- Sugary commercial treats
- Yogurt drops

Rabbits' Shocking Habit

We can't close our chat about rabbit nutrition without talking about one more thing. In the opening of this book, I promised to tell you about rabbits' shocking (but incredible) habit of eating their own poop. It's called *cecotrophy* because the poops that rabbits eat aren't the hard, round pellets we affectionately term "bunny berries." A rabbit's cecum—that large organ that ferments food—produces special droppings called *cecotropes* (pronounced SEE-koh-trohps).

Cecotropes look like small, grayish-brown clusters of grapes. You may rarely see them because most rabbits eat them as they are expelled without letting them get dirty on the cage floor. I know it sounds silly to talk about poop getting dirty, but this habit isn't as gross as it sounds. Cecotrophy is like a cow chewing its cud; by sending food back through the digestive system, rabbits can pull more protein, fat, and nutrients from hay than they could the first time. Packed with vitamin B, vitamin K, amino acids, and beneficial bacteria, cecotropes are basically homemade probiotics and multivitamins for rabbits!

6

A Day in The Life of a Bunny: Everyday Rabbit Care

Keeping a bunny isn't an only-on-the-weekends hobby. Your rabbit needs to eat, drink, and play every day of the week. But there are some rabbit care tasks (like grooming) that you can get away with doing less often.

I find that setting a daily rabbit care routine and a weekly chore schedule helps me stay on track. By nature, I'm a master procrastinator. But if I plan to clean drop trays every Monday, Wednesday, and Saturday, I do it. When I set a schedule, the work gets done, and I don't need to spend extra energy convincing myself it "really needs to happen any day now."

Routine Rabbit Care Schedules

A daily rabbit care routine should include (at a minimum) the tasks listed below.

Example Daily Rabbit Care Routine

- ☐ Feed your rabbit (twice a day).
- ☐ Change its water (twice a day).
- ☐ Observe your rabbit for signs of illness.
- ☐ Check the cage and environment for risks of escape or injury.
- ☐ Clean up any messes that would put the rabbit in direct contact with its droppings or urine.
- ☐ Let your rabbit out to exercise.

Example Weekly Rabbit Care Routine

Monday	Empty drop tray or change litter.
Tuesday	Give bunny a complete health exam.
Wednesday	Empty drop tray or change litter.
Thursday	Inspect cage for maintenance needs.
Friday	Groom and trim nails.
Saturday	Deep clean and sanitize cage, food bowl, and water bottle.
Sunday	Give bunny extra playtime or training.

Cleaning a Rabbit's Environment

Cleaning is the most variable task on our bunny care checklist. How often you'll need to clean depends on your rabbit cage setup. If you have a house rabbit that uses a litter box, you should clean it every day. If you have outdoor rabbits that live in wire cages with drop trays, it's fine to empty the trays two to three times a week, especially if you use shavings or bedding to absorb odors.

Whatever your setup, you need to clean often enough that your rabbit area doesn't smell like urine and your rabbit isn't sitting in its poop.

It's Not Cool to Not Clean

I know we've talked about rabbit poop a lot in this book—and I'm sorry about that. But rabbits make a pile of it every day. And if you don't clean it every day, you'll smell it all the time!

If you have a house rabbit, your family won't take kindly to breathing ammonia or stepping on surprise bunny bombs.

But it's worse for your pet. A dirty cage can make your rabbit really sick. Parasites called

"Fresh water, high-quality hay, and pelleted feed are the foundation for a healthy rabbit. Clean the water bowls daily and always make sure hay is available. A well-ventilated space will prevent respiratory issues."

— **Gina Williams**, Rabbit Habitat

coccidia hatch in rabbit poop. Rabbits that sit in urine-soaked bedding can get painful sores on their legs and hind parts. And, not to give you nightmares, but flies sometimes lay eggs in those sores that hatch into nasty larvae. Ewwwwww!

Cleaning your equipment often also makes it last longer. Rabbit urine is high in calcium. This calcium will coat your cage in a white, rock-like substance if you let it build up.

Bathing Your Rabbit

Maybe you're saying, "Okay, already! I'll clean my rabbit's cage! Should I give my bunny a bath at the same time?"

The surprising answer to this is "no!" You don't need to give your rabbit a bath because bunnies bathe themselves.

Rabbits lick themselves from head to toe every day. They even pull their ears down to clean them—and it's one of the cutest things they do. This meticulous self-grooming usually keeps their coats glossy, smooth, and free of loose fur and debris.

A healthy rabbit coat resists both dirt and water. This is thanks to its structure—made of short, fluffy "underfur" with thick protective top hairs—and the coat's natural oils. If you give your rabbit a bath, even using a "rabbit-safe" shampoo, you can damage the fur structure and strip those healthy oils from the coat. Dunking a rabbit in water can also send it into shock.

When I judge county fairs, I see bunnies whose well-meaning owners gave them baths before bringing them to the show. These poor creatures look remarkably like your old stuffed animals that have been through the dryer too many times—only they're alive. Rabbits aren't meant to take full baths!

Occasionally you may have to give a rabbit a partial bath. If your rabbit is elderly, disabled, or cannot groom itself, it might need help keeping its underparts clean. You can fill a shallow pan with plain room-temperature water and gently work built-up crud out of its fur.

HOW TO REMOVE STAINS FROM RABBIT FUR

If your white rabbit has urine stains on its coat, alcohol is the best way to remove them. Follow these steps:

1. Dip a toothbrush in rubbing alcohol and brush it onto the stained fur.

2. Quickly, before it dries, sprinkle cornstarch onto the fur to absorb the stain.

3. In a few minutes, comb the cornstarch out of the coat. Voila! Clean bunny.

Brushing and Combing Your Rabbit

Most shorthaired rabbits who are between molts don't need frequent grooming. Once a week, just brush their hair in the direction that it grows to keep them looking fabulous.

All rabbits molt—that is, shed a complete coat—once or twice a year. During molts, they can use some extra help to remove loose fur. You can brush your shorthaired rabbit with a wire comb and/or a silicone mitt to help make sure it doesn't swallow too much fur when it grooms itself.

THE UGLY SIDE OF MOLTING...

When rabbits molt, they look terrible. Don't worry; just because their hair is all falling out doesn't mean they are sick!

Longhaired rabbits need more careful and regular grooming. Breeds like the Jersey Wooly, American Fuzzy Lop, and Lionhead have relatively "easy-care" wool. It's longer than regular rabbit hair but coarse in texture and not prone to tangling. Combing these breeds every few days keeps their coats free of debris.

But Angora rabbits have long, soft, luxurious coats that require time-intensive care. If you are drawn to an Angora breed, ask a breeder to give you a grooming tutorial. Then, talk to your parents or family to make sure they understand the commitment.

Cutting Killer Rabbit Claws

Trimming nails seems to be the most intimidating part of rabbit care. Cut those killer rabbit claws? Are you crazy??

But I have a secret for you: It's not that hard. Really. Truly. Believe in yourself. You can learn to trim rabbit nails.

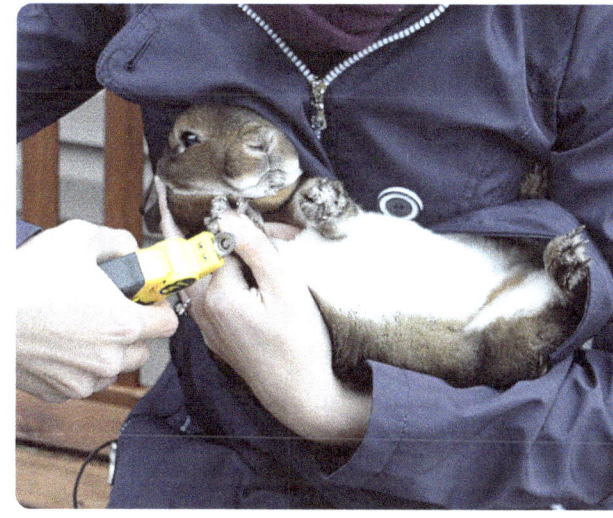

First, you need the right equipment. Always use a nail trimmer intended for animals, not humans. I prefer the "guillotine" style clippers, but other styles can work. You may also want an old towel to wrap the bunny in and some cornstarch or styptic powder to stop bleeding.

Second, know what you're looking for. You don't need to trim the nails down to the toe. Rabbit nails have a blood vessel that extends roughly half an inch out into the nail.

If you place your fingertip into a rabbit's paw, the nails will extend and curl around your finger. Hold them up to the light. Try to see the darker blood vessel in the nail. Aim to cut just beyond it. If you cut the vessel, your bunny will feel pain, and there will be blood. But if you don't cut the vessel, your bunny won't be hurt at all.

The third thing you should know is that the more comfortable you are handling your rabbit in general, the easier nail trimming will become. There's no shame in asking for help holding your rabbit the first few times you trim its nails, but it gets easier with time.

How to Trim Rabbit Nails

When you feel ready, grab a friend, your bunny, and your supplies and sit down in an enclosed area—whether a room in your house or a pen in the grass. You can hold your rabbit upside down to trim its nails, tucking its head under your elbow and resting its body on your lap. This works better for rabbits that are prone to struggle.

If your bunny is calm and used to being handled, you can hold it upright on your lap— wrapped in a towel or not. Then, you can lift one foot at a time to trim its nails.

Whichever position you use, extend the nails by holding the rabbit's ankle and pressing the tip of your thumb into its footpad. Look for the blood vessel and trim just below it. Squeeze the trimmers firmly and release them quickly.

HOW OFTEN SHOULD YOU TRIM A RABBIT'S NAILS?

You should trim your rabbit's nails as often as needed. Rabbits that run around outside wear down their nails faster than rabbits that don't. While there isn't a set rule, you need to trim often so that the nails won't snag and break, potentially breaking your rabbit's toes as well.

If your rabbit starts to struggle, release it and calm it before trying again. (This is why you should always be sitting on the ground when you trim nails.) If a nail bleeds, don't panic! Stop the bleeding with cornstarch, give the bunny a treat, and try again in half an hour.

Believe me, after you've trimmed rabbit nails three or four times, you'll wonder why it seemed so difficult at first!

In Sickness or Health: Keeping Your Rabbit Well

In a sense, keeping your rabbit healthy is not too different from keeping yourself healthy. With good-quality food, exercise, and a clean environment, most pet rabbits stay in great shape.

But there's one major difference between taking care of yourself and taking care of a bunny. If your tummy is upset, or you twist your ankle, or you have tooth pain—you know it. You can tell someone who can get you medication or take you to the doctor. You can, and you should seek help before the problem gets out of control.

If a rabbit has digestive, respiratory, or dental problems, it will try to hide them. In the wild, rabbits that appear weak are most likely to be targeted by predators. If you don't examine your rabbit carefully for signs of illness, it's easy to overlook symptoms until they are so advanced that your rabbit's life is in danger.

Sadly, many serious rabbit diseases don't have safe, effective treatments. Prevention and observation are critical to rabbit health. Read all you can about rabbit diseases so you'll recognize the signs of illness and can call a vet early.

Finding a Good Veterinarian

What's harder to find than a magical unicorn? A good rabbit vet, of course. (Heh, it's almost easier to find a veterinarian who treats unicorns than it is to find one who is experienced with rabbits!)

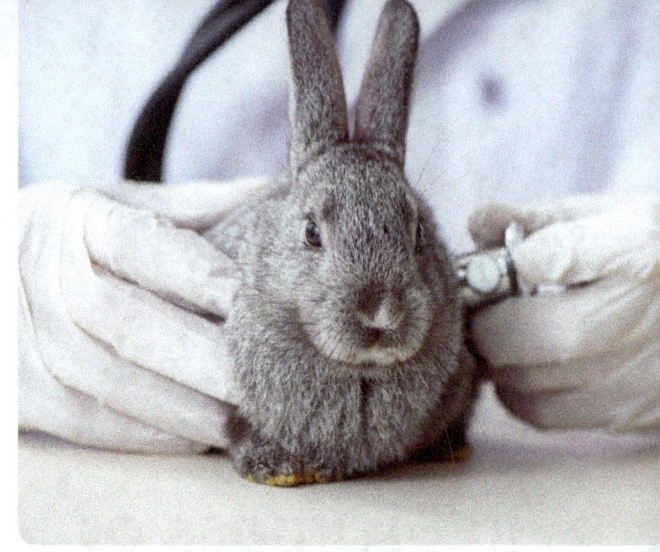

Veterinarians tend to fall into one of three categories. They may be farm vets used to treating livestock. They may be your everyday dog and cat vets. Or they may specialize in "exotics"—which can mean anything from cockatoos to pygmy hedgehogs to bearded dragons.

As you can see, rabbits don't clearly fall into any of these categories. Any of these three types of veterinarians might have experience treating rabbits—or they might not.

Lack of experience is not entirely the vets' fault. Rabbit owners typically don't have a large budget for health care, so most animal doctors don't get a chance to handle a lot of rabbits. But it's discouraging as an owner when your pet needs answers, and your vet can't help you.

When your pet gets sick, you won't have time to call every vet in town to find one that is comfortable treating bunnies. So, you should try to find a rabbit-savvy vet as soon as you get your pet. Take your bunny to the vet's office for a wellness check shortly after you bring it home.

At a wellness check, a vet will look your rabbit over for illness, discuss vaccinations available in your area, and give you a chance to ask questions. Come prepared to ask about treatments for specific diseases and get a feel for the vet's experience with bunnies.

A Rabbit Health Check

After an initial visit, most rabbit owners don't take their bunnies to the vet for yearly check-ups. But whether or not you go to the vet for regular wellness checks, you should examine your rabbit weekly for signs that it's not feeling well.

Use this checklist for your rabbit health exams.

- [ ] **Eyes** should be bright and clear, with no discharge. Check the fur around the eyes for wetness.
- [ ] **Ears** should be clean inside. They should be well-furred, with no bare spots, wounds, or missing chunks. It shouldn't bother the rabbit if you touch them.
- [ ] **Teeth** should show the top incisors overlapping the bottom ones, with no broken teeth. Check lips for abscesses.
- [ ] **Nose** should be dry. Check for discharge (clear, white, or yellow). Watch for very quick breathing or panting.
- [ ] **Head** should be carried straight, not tilted. Feel the skin on the head for abscesses, especially around the ears and jawline.

- [ ] **Genitals and tail** should be clean. No built-up poop, no scabs or sores, no pimples.
- [ ] **Feet and legs** should be straight, covered in clean, dry fur, and free of sores. Watch for matted, worn-away, or dirty fur on the insides of the front legs and the bottoms of the hind feet.
- [ ] **Toenails** — Rabbits should have five nails on each front foot and four on each hind foot. Look for broken nails or toes.
- [ ] **Fur** should be glossy and smooth with no bare batches or scabs on the skin and no visible fleas or mites.
- [ ] **General condition** — The body should feel firm and smooth with no visible bones. You should be able to feel the spine and hip bones, but they shouldn't be sharp or pointed.

- **Posture** can tell you a lot about how a rabbit is feeling. If a bunny's tummy is upset, it will hunch its back and may grind its teeth. If a rabbit is terrified, it will crouch low, poised to run. If it's relaxed, it will lie down or settle into a squishy ball.

- **Demeanor** — Healthy rabbits aren't afraid of humans. They may seek attention, or they may ignore you as they stay busy with their own pursuits. Watch for signs that your rabbit is acting differently from its usual self. Be especially wary of a rabbit hiding in a corner, unwilling to move.

- **Appetite** — If a rabbit stops eating, check its water. Rabbits won't eat if they can't drink. If a rabbit has water but stops eating, you need to treat it as GI stasis.

- **Droppings** should be round, small, hard, and dry. Rabbits poop multiple times every day. If the "bunny berries" stop coming, or if they are mushy or smeary, you should let an adult, a vet, or your rabbit mentor know.

- **Cecotropes** are the soft, dark-green or brown droppings that rabbits typically consume. If you see a few on the cage floor now and then, don't be alarmed.

- **Urine** is often opaque yellow in rabbits due to its high calcium content. Sometimes, it's clear yellow. It can also be reddish if the rabbit eats more protein than it needs. Red urine isn't a sign of illness, but it is a sign that you should adjust your pet's diet. Watch for thick calcium deposits in the urine. If your bunny seems to have difficulty or be in pain when peeing, you should suspect kidney or bladder stones and see a veterinarian.

Common Rabbit Diseases

Let's look at some common categories of rabbit sicknesses. The following isn't even close to a complete list of rabbit diseases! You probably won't be able to diagnose your rabbit yourself just based on this information. But it will give you some signs to look out for so you know when to call a vet or rabbit expert. In the back of this book, you'll find a page that recommends resources so you can study rabbit diseases and treatments in detail.

Respiratory Disease

Catching a cold is miserable for anybody. But for bunnies, respiratory disease is a big deal. If a rabbit is persistently sneezing and wiping snot off its nose, don't expect it to get better on its own in a few days. The first thing you should do is check your bunny's nostrils for bits of stuck hay that could be irritating it. If you don't see any, quarantine the bunny from other rabbits while you consult a vet or rabbit mentor.

Respiratory infections in rabbits are colloquially known as "snuffles." Snuffles is usually caused by bacteria called *Pasteurella multocida*, but it could be from other viruses or bacteria. If you have one pet rabbit, a vet may give you antibiotics for it. However, breeders usually remove rabbits that get snuffles from their herds.

Dental Problems

Rabbits' front teeth can grow a centimeter every month. That's like regrowing the visible part of your front teeth every four weeks!

Lucky bunnies—they don't have to worry about tooth decay in their incisors. But if those front teeth aren't worn down by constant chewing, they can grow so long they poke up through a rabbit's nose!

If you don't want to trim rabbit teeth ('cuz it's way harder than trimming toenails!), never buy a bunny with teeth that aren't lined up correctly. The top teeth should always fully overlap the bottom teeth. Teeth that aren't lined up right are called "buck teeth" or malocclusion.

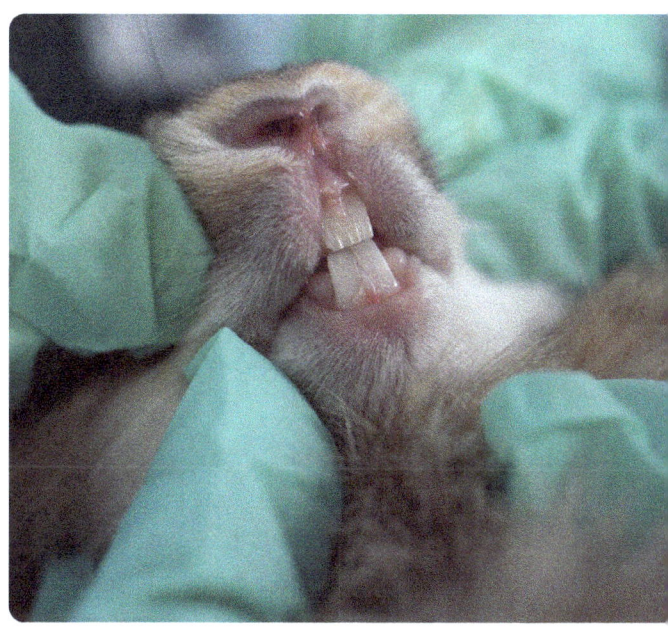

Digestive Problems

As we talked about in Chapter 5, a rabbit's digestive system is happiest when food is constantly moving through it. (Rabbits don't benefit from intermittent fasting like people do!) If the system stops moving because of a poor diet (with not enough fiber) or gets blocked by fur or something indigestible, like carpet threads, your rabbit can become dangerously sick very quickly.

If your rabbit stops eating, stops pooping, has a distended stomach and/or doesn't want to move, or has diarrhea, you should seek a veterinarian's advice right away. A slowed-down digestive tract in a rabbit is called GI stasis. Treatment usually involves force-feeding fluids and electrolytes. High-fiber diets are crucial for prevention.

> "Keep an eye on your rabbit's stool—changes in size or consistency can be a sign of gastrointestinal issues. Early detection is key to preventing serious health problems."
>
> — **Hailee Mihalec**, Stoney Creek Rabbits

Parasites

Rabbits can get a variety of parasites. These could be pinworms they pick up in the grass or mites that burrow inside their ears. Rabbits can get fleas, but it's rare in bunnies that don't live with cats or dogs in the house.

Most parasites are easy to treat with the right medication—but they shouldn't be ignored. A rabbit with internal parasites may have a dull coat with a rough texture and seem skinny even if it's getting enough food. It will have a harder time fighting off other diseases. Rabbits with external fur mites or ear mites may have bare or bleeding skin from scratching themselves.

WHAT ARE PARASITES?

Parasites are organisms like worms, mites, or fleas that live on or inside a rabbit, feeding off them. These pests can cause health issues such as a dull coat, weight loss, and skin irritation, and they require treatment to prevent further complications.

Viral Diseases

Most rabbit respiratory diseases are caused by bacteria, not viruses. But do rabbits get viruses? Well, as far as scientists can tell, rabbits don't get COVID-19. But there are a couple of serious rabbit viruses that should be on your radar.

Myxomatosis

The first is myxomatosis. This is a pox virus that causes swellings and other symptoms. Myxomatosis is most common in Europe and Australia. In those countries, pet rabbits are regularly vaccinated against the disease. We don't have a vaccine for myxomatosis in the United States.

Thankfully, there have been only occasional outbreaks in North America, usually along the West Coast. This disease is usually spread by insects, so protecting your pet from biting flies is your best defense if you live near an outbreak.

Rabbit VHD

The second disease goes by the acronym RHDV2. This disease is so devastating that Australian scientists used a version of this virus to wipe out rabbits that were destroying crops. This disease first appeared in the United States in the early months of 2020. (Right when we all went into lockdown for other reasons!) Outbreaks since then have been few and spread out, but experts expect them to continue.

There is good news. At the time I wrote this book, the US Department of Agriculture granted emergency permission to veterinarians to import the RHDV2 vaccine from Europe and use it on North American rabbits. Talk with your vet about whether they have access to the vaccine and whether your bunny is likely to need it.

(And, no, you can't get either of these diseases from your rabbit. Just in case your mom was wondering.)

Your Rabbit's Secret Weapon

Your bunny may be a superhero. But he can't stay healthy alone. Like all superheroes, rabbits have their weaknesses.

Your bunny needs you.

You are your rabbit's defender, and your help is its secret weapon. Your bunny desperately needs your care, knowledge, and close attention to complete his mission safely. Be ready. 😊

8

It's Playtime! How to Handle, Train, and Bond with Your Rabbit

At the preschool my kids attend, the teachers call the children's play "work." It sounds funny, but there's a reason behind it. Play makes children grow and stay strong, mentally and physically. For children, play is work.

Rabbits are the same way. When a rabbit is frantically digging in its nest box and rearranging pieces of its straw nest, is it working, or is it playing? Really, it's doing both.

Bunnies are healthiest when they have something constructive to do. This could be gnawing on a branch, grooming another rabbit, or rearranging every wood shaving in its territory. You can place toys, chewing blocks, digging boxes, and/or tunnels in your rabbit's environment to keep it busy while you aren't there. Then, when you're home, you can build a friendship with your bunny. You can explore what kind of petting it likes or direct its energy into learning how to do tricks and jump hurdles.

Trust is a "Must"

Your rabbit won't feel safe showing you its personality until after it has settled into its new home and learned to trust you. Some extroverted rabbits act like the boss from day one and enjoy playtime and pettings right away. But most bunnies take days or weeks after moving to feel comfortable in their new environment and bond with their owners.

> "I like to sit down in a small room with my rabbits and allow them to approach me. Once they feel safe, they become curious and start to explore. Offering treats during these visits can help make the bonding experience fun and safe."
>
> — **Dawn Swanson**, Fox and Crow Farm

"Bonding" with your bunny means helping it learn to trust you. Once you've proven to a rabbit that you're a safe part of its world, your bunny may reward you by sitting on your lap, licking your hand, or inviting you to play.

More importantly, your rabbit will be free to be itself around you. You'll get to see hilarious expressions of bunny emotion like wild binky jumps where your happy rabbit might literally bounce off the walls.

Bonding With a Rabbit — How to Make Your Bunny Trust You

The number one rule when bonding with a rabbit is to go slowly.

When you first bring your rabbit home, give it lots of quiet space. Don't handle it at all in the first few days. Avoid shouting or sudden movements around your bunny—even if that means asking your siblings to "please go play monster trucks in another room—please!??"

If the rabbit's cage is on the floor of your home, set up an exercise pen around the cage and sit inside it. Open the cage door. Don't force your rabbit out of its cage until it's ready. Just sit or lie on the floor and observe.

When your bunny decides to come out, let it sniff or nuzzle you or even nibble you just a bit. Rabbits taste things to learn about them, but they rarely full-on bite. Don't try to grab or hold your bunny while it's investigating you. Don't yell, jump, or panic, even if your bunny gently uses its tongue or teeth.

When you do pet your rabbit, hold your hands out low to the floor and let your bunny smell them first. Stroke its forehead, and if it likes that, continue back along its ears, back, and sides. Don't try to touch its tummy, feet, or tail.

> "Talk to your rabbit and spend time playing with them daily. A rabbit's trust is earned through consistency and calm, reassuring interactions. Start slow and gradually increase handling."
>
> — **Katie Finch**, Leon River Rabbitry

You can encourage your bunny to come to you by holding a treat. Don't jam the snack into your bunny's nose. Instead, keep your hand at ground level and let the rabbit come try the treat when it wants to.

Never use your hands to swoop down on your rabbit like a hawk. Bunnies absolutely hate that—for obvious reasons. Bonding is all about proving to your bunny that you're not a predator.

Then, once your rabbit is convinced that you have no plans to eat it, don't be surprised if your bunny treats you like its slave. "Pet me, human!" it might seem to demand. "Give me snacks—now!"

It's actually really cute.

Rabbit Body Language

The noises rabbits make are soft and infrequent. But bunnies communicate volumes through their body language. The longer you watch your rabbit move, and the more you learn its body language, the faster you will bond with your bunny.

Positive Body Language

Licking and Nuzzling — When a rabbit licks you, it's not trying to taste salt on your skin. It's accepting you into its community. If your rabbit licks you and then places its head on the floor, it wants you to rub him in return.

Binky — This is the high-flying jump for joy that seems to sneak up on rabbits who are running for fun. They may spring straight up or sideways, then land confused, as if saying, "Who did that!? Me?!"

Chinning — Rabbits have scent glands under their chins. When they rub their chin on an object—or a person—they're marking it as an official part of their dominion.

Bunny Loaf and Flopping — Relaxed, comfortable bunnies will sit nestled with their feet tucked under them in a "broody hen" or "bunny loaf" position. Really lazy rabbits will flop over on their sides and lie stretched out on the floor. This position means your rabbit feels fully safe and happy.

Negative Body Language

Feet Flicking — If you annoy your rabbit, you may get the "feet flick" treatment. Your bunny will hop away from you, giving an extra shake to its hind feet in disgust. Don't worry. Its wrath won't last for long.

Cowering and Stamping — A truly frightened rabbit will crouch low to the floor, eyes wide with whites showing. It may stamp a hind foot loudly. When you hear this, stay calm and look for danger, like rats or snakes, especially if your rabbit lives outside.

Biting and Lunging — Most pet rabbits never bite. When they do, they'll usually warn you first. They may grunt, growl, or box at you with their forepaws. They'll flatten their ears against their skulls and show their teeth. If a new rabbit acts aggressively, keep your hands far out of its space. If the behavior doesn't improve in a couple of weeks, you may need to rehome him with an expert and find another bunny.

If you have a rabbit that's normally sweet but suddenly starts biting, take note. This could be a sign that it's sick and trying to hide it.

Do Bunnies Make Noise?

Bunnies are quiet animals, but definitely not silent! Newborn rabbits squeak. Adult bunnies make happy chattering sounds with their teeth. They grunt to ask for something or to show anger. They express excitement with nasal honks. Rabbits scream when terrified—and the sound will stand your hair on end.

But most rabbit sounds are pleasant and comforting. The sounds of my house rabbit contentedly chewing hay, shredding cardboard, or clucking to himself feel like a daily reminder that everything's gonna be okay.

Why You Should Pick Up Your Rabbit

Part of bonding with your rabbit is learning to pick it up. Picking up a rabbit is like learning to trim its toenails. It's a little scary at first, but if you practice, you'll get good at it quickly.

Some people say that you should avoid picking your rabbit up. They say rabbits think they're about to be eaten every time they're lifted off the ground.

> "When you bring your new bunny home, it's important to take things slow. Spending time with them at their level, rather than picking them up immediately, allows them to build trust at their own pace."
>
> — **Heather Epps**, FlowerTown Rabbits

I don't think that's true. If you've proven to your rabbit that you're trustworthy, it won't think you morphed into a monster if you pick it up. My bunnies will run to me and ask to be picked up if they sense danger.

In fact, learning to handle your rabbit is essential for its safety. Imagine if a dog were to chase your bunny. You would need to be able to grab it quickly. You need to be able to hold your rabbit securely when you move it from place to place and avoid injury if it struggles. You need to take your rabbit out and check it for illness every week.

Ultimately, your rabbit will be happier and safer if you practice holding it.

How to Pick Up a Rabbit

Always pick up your rabbit from underneath. Place one hand under its forelegs, cradling its chest. Place your other hand under its rump. Holding firmly, bring the rabbit to your chest. You can hold the rabbit on your chest, keeping both hands on the bunny. Or you can tuck its head under one of your arms and carry it like a football.

The easiest way to learn these motions is to have someone show you, either in person or on YouTube. You'll get better the more you practice. When I was a kid, I had a plush rabbit of a realistic size and shape, and I used to practice all my rabbit wrangling techniques on this bunny. In my room. Alone. For hours. No shame.

Because when you get really good at picking your rabbit up, you can show off your skills in a competition called rabbit showmanship! More on that in the next chapter.

You can hold the rabbit on your chest, keeping both hands on the bunny.

For now, remember these most important rules for handling bunnies.

Rabbit Handling Do's and Don'ts

- Don't ever pick a rabbit up by the skin on the back of its neck. This is called "scruffing." Mama cats may carry their kittens this way, but mama rabbits don't. Rabbit skin and muscles can tear if you carry a bunny like that.

- Don't lift a rabbit by its ears or hips, either. Always support its weight from the underside.

Don't ever pick up your rabbit by the neck!

- Do drop to your knees if a rabbit you're carrying starts to struggle. It's better to lower the bunny to a safe distance from the floor and regain control than risk it jumping or falling out of your arms.

- Do keep the rabbit's feet secure at all times. Rabbits feel safest when all four of their feet are touching something solid.

- Don't let very young kids pick up your rabbit. If a small child wants to hold a rabbit, I will usually wrap the bunny in a towel and place it on the child's lap while the child sits on the floor.

- Do stay calm, even if your rabbit doesn't.

Training Your Rabbit

I've had to face the fact that rabbits will never learn as many tricks as a dog can. Rabbits simply don't care as much about pleasing humans as dogs do!

But they can learn a few tricks! Let's take a quick look at some ways you can train a rabbit.

Litter Training

Rabbits can learn to use a potty just like a toddler—and they'll be about as accurate. Your rabbit may have an accident or two, especially if it isn't spayed or neutered. But since most rabbits always go in one corner of their cage anyway, teaching your pet to use the litter box is fairly simple.

Clicker Training

All you need to teach rabbits tricks is a plan, a treat, and a clicker. A "clicker" is a training tool that makes a distinct sound when you push its button. (Though you can make a similar sound with your tongue instead.)

To teach your rabbit a trick, say a command and encourage your rabbit to perform the activity. (For example, stand on its hind legs or jump through a hoop.) As quickly as you can after the rabbit does the trick, make the clicking sound and reward your bunny with a treat. It will catch on pretty quickly.

Rabbit Hopping/Agility

If you have a young, active bunny that responds well to clicker training, it might be a candidate for competitive rabbit hopping!

Did you know that people teach their bunnies to jump high hurdles and navigate agility courses? Yeah? Well, more on that coming up next.

9

Take Me Out to the Rabbit Show.

I think I mentioned that my husband and I had our first date at a rabbit show. We didn't *meet* at a rabbit show; he wasn't a rabbit guy back then. I dragged him along. But rabbit shows were my natural habitat, so I was basically just bringing him home.

A rabbit show is a great place to bring your boyfriend or other people unfamiliar with the rabbit world. There, you get to show them all the breeds of rabbits and hear their reactions. "Whoa! I had no idea rabbits could get so big!" or "Look at that stunning black and red rabbit!" or "Where even is the bunny under all that fluff?"

A rabbit show often takes place in a big old barn where rabbit owners gather to meet friends, trade rabbits, and compare their carefully groomed bunnies to other ones. Judges award prizes to the prettiest rabbits, to the best jumpers, and to kids who have studied lots about bunnies and taken great care of their animals.

Rabbit shows happen all over the country, but they are more common in certain regions.

Is Showing Rabbits Right for You?

It all sounds great. But rabbit shows aren't for everyone. You might be happier just keeping a pet bunny and not taking him to a show. Let's look at some pros and cons of showing your rabbit.

Benefits of Showing Your Rabbit

+ You meet people who can support and mentor you on your rabbit journey.
+ You get to see lots of different breeds and colors of bunnies.
+ It can be a great family activity to do with your parents, grandparents, or siblings.
+ There's a chance to compete and win ribbons.
+ It's a great way to build confidence and gives you a goal to work toward.

Drawbacks of Showing Your Rabbit

- ✘ It's expensive. Shows take a lot of time and money. When I was a teen, I sold rabbit-themed books and products at shows to cover travel costs and entry fees.
- ✘ Your rabbit could catch a disease from other rabbits at the show.
- ✘ Showing draws the focus away from simply enjoying your bunny and its personality.
- ✘ It's easy to get caught up in competition. But winning at shows may take years of time and practice. You may be disappointed if you don't win.
- ✘ Showing makes you want more rabbits!

Looking back at my childhood, I'm now amazed and thankful that my parents took me to rabbit shows. They're such a big commitment! A regular rabbit show takes up a whole Saturday. Then, if you show at the county fair, you may need to go feed your rabbit every day while it stays there for a whole week.

The good part is that if you and your family decide you want to try rabbit shows, the level of commitment is flexible. You can show your rabbit every weekend, or just once a year, or something in between.

The Clubs Come First

It takes a lot of people to plan and host a rabbit show. That's why every rabbit show is sponsored by a rabbit club. Some clubs are organized through the American Rabbit Breeders Association (ARBA) and include adult members. Others are 4-H clubs just for kids.

In the United States, there are three main types of rabbit shows. The type is determined by the group that's hosting it.

1. ARBA-sanctioned shows
2. 4-H shows
3. County fairs (May be associated with 4-H or with the local FFA chapter.)

What to Expect at a Rabbit Show

Shows hosted by ARBA clubs tend to be bigger, more expensive, and more competitive. You can find a list of these shows on the ARBA website, www.ARBA.net.

American Rabbit Breeders Association

4-H rabbit shows are sponsored by local 4-H clubs. The atmosphere is more chill at these events, and they often have a variety of contests or games for kids to participate in. 4-H shows are great places to test the waters of the competitive rabbit world.

To find 4-H shows, search online for "extension office" in your county and ask them about local rabbit clubs and shows.

The third kind of show is a county fair. Rabbits are usually kept in cages at the fair for several days. Fairs keep bunnies on display so the general public that comes to the fair to go to the demolition derby or the carnival can also walk goggle-eyed through a barn full of rabbits. Fairs emphasize learning about rabbit care, so kids usually decorate the rabbit barn with educational posters.

But what happens at a rabbit show? And how does the judge pick the winning bunny? Well, there are a few different ways this happens.

Breed Confirmation Classes vs. Youth Contests

Before I could drive, my dad took me to rabbit shows. And at every one, he'd grab some other parent and drone his standard line, "I don't understand it. We tell our kids we love them no matter how they look—and then we take them to rabbit shows, where only the prettiest bunny wins."

Sometimes I'd get defensive and say,

"DAAAD, THAT'S NOT THE ONLY THING THAT MATTERS!"

> "The bond formed between you and your rabbit is the foundation for any successful show. The more trust your rabbit has in you, the more relaxed they will be during handling and judging."
>
> — **Stephanie Parker**, Hoppy Trails Rabbitry

But actually, he was right—at least in some cases.

The shows where the prettiest bunny wins are called breed confirmation classes. The ARBA publishes a book that describes the ideal body shape, color pattern, and coat texture for each breed. Judges award rabbits prizes based on which bunny looks most like the description in the book.

But thankfully, for kids under 19, that's not the only way you can win prizes. There are several other contests you can participate in, especially at 4-H shows and fairs. Contests like showmanship and royalty test your rabbit knowledge and handling. They test your skills and aren't dependent on how cute and fluffy your bunny looks that day.

Showmanship

The most popular of these youth contests is called showmanship. Showmanship was fun because (at least in my day) you styled your hair and wore a white lab coat.

However you dress in a showmanship contest, you will need to prove to the judge that you know how to pose your rabbit, carry it safely, and turn it over. You will need to answer questions about rabbit health and feeding.

SHOWMANSHIP

Smile and make eye contact with the judges. They're looking for a confident young professional who embodies the cheerful spirit of the rabbit hobby.

"Start working with your rabbit at least several months before the show. Practice posing your rabbit regularly, ensuring they are comfortable with the show table. This builds confidence and allows the rabbit to become familiar with being handled."

— **Gina Williams**, Rabbit Habitat

Judging

In a judging competition, you roleplay being a rabbit judge. You will evaluate four rabbits and place them first to last based on the ARBA Standard of Perfection. Your placement is compared to the placement of licensed adult judges.

JUDGING

Check every rabbit for disqualifications before starting to evaluate them. Rabbits with disqualifications should be placed last.

Breed Identification

Breed Identification was my personal favorite competition. Unlike judging, "breed ID" isn't subjective. There's a right and a wrong answer that's consistent every time. In breed ID, you look at 20 to 30 rabbits and identify their breed and exact color variety. It's trickier than it sounds!

Rabbit Royalty

Royalty is kind of like a Miss Universe pageant for rabbit breeders. Kind of not. But you do get a sash and a tiara if you win.

Royalty is a multistage competition that includes a written application, a test, an interview, and some hands-on rabbit skill demonstrations. The winners, depending on age, are crowned "King" or "Queen," "Prince" or "Princess," and "Duke" or "Duchess."

BREED ID

Memorize the recognized colors of every breed. You won't mistake an Otter Britannia Petite for a Polish if you remember that Polish don't come in the color otter.

ROYALTY

Have fun with it. There are so many factors that affect the final score in royalty that it's impossible to predict a winner. Enjoy the experience and make friends with the other contestants.

Rabbit Hopping and Agility

Competitive rabbit jumping started in Sweden, where it goes by the adorable name of Kaninhoppning. It spread to North America only in the last decade or two.

In rabbit show jumping, bunnies leap over hurdles that look like mini horse jumps. These obstacles typically range up to 20 inches high or 30 inches long.

Rabbit agility is based on dog agility competitions. Rabbits run an obstacle course that involves hopping, climbing ramps, and going through tunnels. In both agility and hopping, rabbits stay on a harness, and the owner runs alongside them.

You don't need fancy equipment to train your rabbit to hop! Search the web for great DIY obstacle ideas.

HOPPING

Make sure the harness is tight enough! Rabbits' fluffiness makes them look bigger than they are, so they can slip right out of the harness if it's not fitted to the skin. And never use a collar and leash that only circle the rabbit's neck.

Other Competitions

That's not all! The ones described above are only a few of the contests that the ARBA and 4-H clubs offer young rabbit owners. Depending on your area, shows may have quiz bowls, skill-a-thons, craft contests, or other activities.

The ARBA Convention

I can't complete our chapter on rabbit shows without inviting you to the biggest rabbit show ever!

It's called the ARBA National Convention, and it can draw as many as 20,000 rabbits and their owners. The location moves around the country from year to year, but it's almost always held in October.

ARBA Convention Highlights

- Seeing new breeds and colors still in development or imported from other countries
- A dramatic Best in Show ceremony
- Royalty, breed ID, and other competitions
- Banquets and dances—including one just for youth
- Shopping at dozens of rabbit-themed vendor booths
- The chance to talk about nothing but rabbits for days on end

You can participate in the ARBA convention even if you can't attend! The ARBA has several mail-in contests for young members that involve writing, T-shirt design, or other creative work. Check out the ARBA website for details.

10

Rabbits and Your Future: The Impact of Rabbit Keeping

Did you know that keeping bunnies isn't just personally rewarding? There are lots of exciting ways that your rabbit can make a positive difference in the community around you.

How Can Rabbits Benefit Your Community?

Here are a few ideas for how you and your bunnies can team up and use your collective superpowers for the common good.

Emotional Support and Therapy Bunnies

Bunnies brighten everyone's day! Ask if your rabbit can accompany you on a visit to a nursing home or a retirement center to encourage the residents there. You can also contact groups that bring therapy animals into children's hospitals and ask how to get involved.

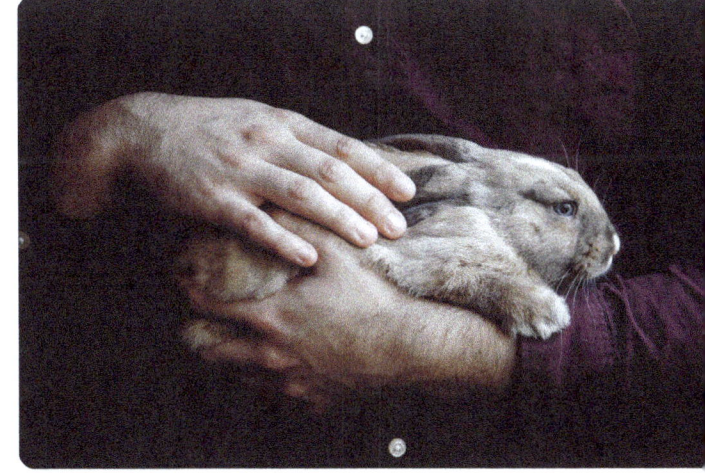

Of course, any rabbit that takes a job as a therapy animal needs to have a gentle personality, enjoy being held, and be very well trained. You must keep your bunny's nails trimmed and handle it frequently if it's going to be an emotional support animal. Some bunnies are better suited to this kind of work than others.

Workshops for Kids

Call your local petting zoo or park district and offer to teach a workshop on keeping rabbits for kids! These classes are especially popular around Easter time. You can prepare a short presentation on how to take care of a rabbit, along with printed handouts, activities, educational games, and prizes. Make sure to include time for children to pet a bunny or take a photo with it and allow parents to ask questions.

Fiber Production

If you have an Angora rabbit with long, fluffy wool, you can hack your inner Laura Ingalls and spin that wool into yarn! You can use the yarn to knit some of the softest, warmest socks, hats, or mittens and donate them to community shelters or people in need.

Community Agriculture

Rabbits are not just pets—they also have an important place in agriculture. Rabbits fit perfectly into the life cycle of a small homestead or community garden. They can eat garden scraps—like overgrown lettuce, cast-off cucumbers, or squash leaves—and then turn them into one of the best fertilizers found in nature.

As grocery prices climb higher and higher, more people are looking to meat rabbits as a source of food for their families. You can work with local farms, high schools, or colleges to provide classes or resources on keeping meat rabbits. You can work to increase public awareness that rabbit meat is one of the healthiest and most humanely raised animal proteins available.

True Impact Takes Teamwork

If these ideas for serving your community through your rabbit project have you hopping like a Belgian Hare, then I'm very excited with you! But I have one important reminder to share: you can be most effective if you work with a group!

And so we return to rabbit clubs. Clubs are the backbone of the rabbit community. Not every local 4-H or ARBA club is involved in community service, but many are, and others just need some new energy to get the ball rolling.

If you don't find a local club near you at all, then you have two options: start your own club or turn to an online network.

When I was a kid, I started my own rabbit club with my church and a local homeschool group. It wasn't affiliated with any larger organization, but we had a lot of fun hosting unofficial shows, creating newsletters, and helping the public learn about bunny care.

These days, there are online rabbit groups and forums where you can connect with other rabbit keepers, share ideas, receive encouragement, ask questions, learn a lot, and make friends. Of course, even rabbit groups are never 100% safe online, so always interact with these forums with the guidance of an adult.

Rabbit World Friendships Could Last Forever

The best part of rabbit-keeping communities, whether online or in-person, is the friendships you make. I'm not close to many of my school friends anymore, but I have rabbit-world friends from childhood who are still a major part of my life.

You'll also forge other relationships through the rabbit world that can be building blocks to your career. Perhaps you can start a side hustle watching other people's rabbits; those people could be references for your first "real job." There's a good chance your 4-H leader will write you a letter of recommendation for a scholarship application when you go to college. In fact, involvement, leadership, and accomplishments in the rabbit community will always look great on scholarship applications!

The people you meet through raising rabbits become your tribe, your network. They are the people through whom doors will open to lead wherever life will take you.

Rabbits and Your Future

Once a bunny lover, always a bunny lover. If you make the most of your relationship with your rabbit as a kid, there's a high chance that your experience with rabbit keeping will impact your adult life.

You might become a vet or an animal nutritionist. You might be a kindergarten teacher and keep a rabbit in the classroom. You might end up with a career in a totally unrelated field, but always come home to recharge with a pet bunny or three hopping around your feet.

Or maybe you'll be a globetrotting digital nomad, so you can't keep a real rabbit, but you'll collect bunny figurines from around the world instead. Because once bunnies have burrowed into your heart, they'll always have a special place there.

Note for Parents and Teachers

Dear Parents, Guardians, and Teachers,

A rabbit is a great choice for the first pet to entrust to your child. Rabbits are adorable, intelligent, and social animals that can bring joy and companionship to your family.

However, rabbits are also complex creatures that require special care and attention. They are not toys or accessories that can be left alone in a cage all day. They need a proper diet, a spacious and safe environment, regular exercise, social interaction, and veterinary care.

This book is designed to help your child learn about the basic needs and behaviors of rabbits, as well as how to interact with them in a respectful and responsible way. It also explores some ways your child can broaden their horizons in the rabbit hobby, such as competing in rabbit agility, joining rabbit clubs, or encouraging people in your community to explore rabbit ownership. These sorts of ideas can light a fire under ambitious kids and give them a positive outlet for their creative energy.

However, your child will need guidance on every step of their rabbit-keeping adventure. Young children may need to learn to speak and move gently to build a relationship with their bunny. Caring for a small animal means your child may have to process difficult or delicate realities of life and death.

If, as a family, you do move into the rabbit clubs, showing, or business circuits, your child will have to learn to handle financial decisions, how to balance their investment of time with potential rewards and risks of disappointment, and how to work with people in a group setting. All of these things are hugely valuable life skills, but your child will need your help to grow in these areas.

I want to encourage you, however, that the rewards of getting involved in the rabbit industry are great. Many rabbit clubs, including the American Rabbit Breeders Association, offer scholarships and mentorship opportunities for young people.

I grew up with many friends in the rabbit world who built careers on their rabbit hobby connections. I won't use their real names, but here are a few examples.

- **Josh** became an accountant for an international animal nutrition corporation.
- **Katelyn** became a lobbyist for small-scale farmers and, in her spare time, travels to third-world nations as a consultant for organizations building community-supported rabbit farming projects.
- **Brent** is a high school teacher, mentoring students who raise rabbits through the school's FFA program. On weekends, he's a rabbit judge. He's been invited to judge rabbit shows in 47 states and five different nations.
- **Stacey** uses her experiences as a homesteader to run a successful social media channel and teach her three kids the value of self-sufficiency.

The best part about being involved in the broader rabbit hobby is that you'll meet lots of people who are happy to answer your questions about bunny keeping and become supportive friends. Please see the next section of this book, "Resources," for information on how to find rabbit clubs near you.

Wishing you the best in this journey!

Resources for Further Learning

American Rabbit Breeders Association (ARBA)
www.arba.net

The American Rabbit Breeders Association publishes six issues a year of Domestic Rabbits, a magazine filled with the latest research and helpful articles from veteran rabbit keepers. The ARBA website is the best place to find rabbit shows near you. Your regional ARBA district director can help you connect with other rabbit breeders in your area. The ARBA also hosts the largest rabbit show in the world, the annual ARBA Convention.

Find Your Local 4-H Club Through the 4-H Website
www.4-h.org/about/find/

Visit the official 4-H website to locate clubs and rabbit-related programs near you. Discover opportunities to connect, learn, and grow with 4-H!

Fuzzy-Rabbit.com
www.fuzzy-rabbit.com

One of the most up-to-date and complete resources on pet rabbit care, this website focuses on pet-care aspects of rabbit keeping, including litter box training and bonding with your rabbit.

Rabbit Smarties
www.rabbitsmarties.com

This author's blog is full of resources and study guides for kids interested in rabbit showmanship or other competitions.